LATIN chic

CAROLINA BUIA AND ISABEL C. GONZÁLEZ

PHOTOGRAPHS BY JIM FRANCO

rayo *An Imprint of* HarperCollins *Publishers*

LATIN chic

Entertaining with Style and Sass

HarperCollins books may be purchased for educational, business, or sales
promotional use. For information, please write: Special Markets Department,
HarperCollins Publishers, 10 East 53rd Street, New York, NY 10022.

FIRST EDITION

BOOK DESIGN BY SHUBHANI SARKAR
PHOTOGRAPHS BY JIM FRANCO

Printed on acid-free paper

Library of Congress Cataloging-in-Publication Data
Buia, Carolina.
    Latin chic: entertaining with style and sass / Carolina Buia and
    Isabel González.—1st ed.
      p. cm.
    ISBN 0-06-073871-5
    1. González, Isabel (Isabel C.)   II. Title.
  TX723.B769   2005
  642'.4-dc22   2005041076

05 06 07 08 09 ❖/TOP 10 9 8 7 6 5 4 3 2 1

This book is lovingly dedicated to our MOMS and DADS.
When you came to this country,
you brought Latin style and sensibility.
This book is, in part, an homage to your world.

And thanks to our wonderful husbands,
HEATH BAREFOOT and **LANG WHITAKER**,
who tested recipes, edited copy,
and provided endless love and support.

contents

acknowledgments

WE ARE INDEBTED to many people who helped make this book possible:

Jim Franco, our talented photographer, lent his patience, dedication, and vision to this project. Joe Maer, prop stylist *extraordinario,* was invaluable throughout our numerous shoots. As was Jee Levin, our fabulous food stylist.

Gareth Edmonson-Jones at JetBlue not only helped get many of our shoots off the ground (literally), but also became a great friend. Thanks to him and the JetBlue team, including Todd Burke, Bryan Baldwin, and Clare Kiikka, we flew to many beautiful places. Also, a thank-you to the folks at Eastman Kodak Company for believing in the importance of this project.

Thanks also to Ines Segarra of the Argentine Tourism Office in New York, Rose Mary Cortes with the Mexican Tourism Board, and Glorimar Alvarez at the Puerto Rican Tourism Board. The talented duo of Nicole Fernandez of Uncharted Outposts and Maita Barrenechea of Maiten planned our fabulous trip to Argentina and helped us negotiate our way (and our cameras) through customs. Claudio Silvestri, Emilia Fanjul, Kim Hutchinson, Sandra Lopez, and Angel Pacheco organized the most romantic weekend at Casa de Campo in the Dominican Republic. Holly Blount opened the doors and grounds of the lovely Vizcaya Museum and Gardens in Miami. And we say thank you to the numerous other people who supported our project, including Bill Baites, of Miami Beach's Tourism and Cultural Development Office; Heather Zaitz, at the National Hotel in Miami; Natalia Zaldivar, at Victor's Café; Kelly Vogt, at the St. Regis in Los Angeles; Orlando Hidalgo, at the Hosteria Las Quintas Eco Spa in Cuernavaca; Paulina Cornejo Moreno-Valle, at the Centro Cultural Muros Museum in Cuernavaca; Leslie Arvelo, at the Water Club in Puerto Rico; Ruben Rodriguez, of LQ Nightclub in Manhattan; and Jules Haimovitz, who loaned us his guesthouse in Los Angeles.

To the talented Latin designers who provided us with our ultrachic wardrobe for our parties: Carmen Marc Valvo, Angel Sanchez, Sully Bonnelly, Oscar de la Renta, Carolina Herrera, Narciso Rodriguez, Carlos Miele, Amir Slama for Rosa Cha, Edmundo Castillo, Alvin Valley, Pablo Ramirez, and Richard Cohen for Conquete. And to the amazing associates who helped as well, including Frank Pulice, Alexandra Kimball, Daphna Barzilay, Ward H. Simmons, and Veronika Borchers.

Much love to the makeup artists and hair stylists who worked on this book, not only beautifying the models but providing great insight and support: Jesus Abreu, Willie Rosado, Jairo Zuleta, Sara Johnson, and Veronica Lane.

We also must thank Nicole Ehrbar of Cartier and Nicole Bender of Williams-Sonoma for their lovely baubles and tablewares. For the beautiful faces in Miami, thank you Michele Pommier Management, Elite Models, and Next Models. In Puerto Rico, we must thank Elements Models and Unica. In Los Angeles, we are indebted to the Esquire House.

Marilu Menendez gets our gratitude on two counts: for lending her expertise on Latin culture and for her contributions as public relations director for Lord & Taylor, providing clothes for many of our shoots.

Where would we be were it not for the many friends and family members who graciously volunteered to test so many of the recipes in this book? Edith Whitaker, mother-in-law and master baker; Heath Barefoot tackled marine life; Lang Whitaker wrestled the grill; Dori Thompson, master saucier; Ofelia de la Valette and Melissa Buia patiently tested meat dishes while Claire Whitaker and Anabelle de Gale tried vegetarian specialties. And to the rest of our recipe testers: Michelle Hainer and Nancy Beiles (who both lent their eyes for some last-minute copyediting), Eric Dorsch, Chay Avera, Sara González, Fernando González, Seth and Yana Coren, Gina Arias, Cesar and Montserrat Buia, and Ben Baumohl. And a big hug to Marianna Greenlee and Blanca González, both friends and professional cooks who were kind enough to test so many of our dishes.

Thank you also Jennifer Nieman-Abad; Dayanara Torres; Ines Rivero and Jorge Mora; Deborah Carthy-Deu; the Suter famil; Chef Katsuya Fukushima of Café Atlantico and Chef Johnny Iuzzini of Jean-Georges; Perla M. Kuhn; Sandy Fernández; Ana Mollinedo Mims; José Pérez-Aguilera; Miky and Leticia Grendene; Sohali Holland; Lisa Palma; Carmen R. Wong; Aida Flamm; Bernadette Brennan; Claudio Cofré; Isolde Motley; Angelo Figueroa; Luis de la Valette; Christian Buia; Isabel Rivera; Rudi Forster; Patrik Henry Bass; Harvey Levin; Shant Petrossian; Macarena Llambí de Gravière; George Russell; Ezra Marcus; Giselle Fernandez; Sandra González; Daniela Serra; Diana Martinez; Sandra Font; Evan Narcisse; Roger Swain of Kumquat Growers Inc.; Dominque and Michael J. Galluzzi; Palacios de Jugos in Miami; Taylor Foster; Carmen Letscher; Jacqueline Buckingham; Kevin Allyn; Christopher Coleman; Rachel Pringle; Mike Owen and Tara Litwin; Reid Whitaker; Bob and Iris Barefoot; Tias Mercedita Pujol, Sara Paz, and Emma González Azqueta; Abuela Enriqueta Camps Vives and Avi Antonio Camps; Tieta Antonieta Vives; Amy Tan; and Nonna Maria Buia.

Finally, a few New Yorkers who embraced us and our book proposal from the start. They are our fabulous agent, Claudia Cross, who guided us with wisdom, patience, and savvy; our brilliant publisher, Rene Alegria, who believed in this book from the moment we told him about it; book designer Shubhani Sarkar, jacket designer Mumtaz Mustafa, and associate publisher Raymond Garcia; and, of course, the inimitable Harriet Bell, our editorial supermama: we cannot gush enough about her passion for good times, Latin food, and honest writing. Thank you all.

Bienvenidos a **LATIN** chic

Five years ago, we were introduced at a party in midtown Manhattan and couldn't believe how much we had in common. Aside from working in the same building for different magazines (New York is small that way), we shared parallel childhoods, growing up in the United States in Latin households—Carolina is Venezuelan and grew up in Miami, and Isabel is Cuban and grew up in Atlanta. In no time we became fast friends and began an odyssey to explore and celebrate our Latin roots. We began sampling drinks and recipes in our kitchens and soon started inviting our friends to cocktail parties, dinners, brunches, and full-scale fiestas, where we'd always put a Latin twist on things. We mixed and matched dishes from South America and Central America, such as Ecuadorian ceviche served on pretty seashells and Mexican *cochinita pibil* wrapped in iceberg lettuce. We taught our guests the proper way to smoke a cigar and how to play dominoes. We shook up drinks like Bolivian yugeños and came up with our own version of the Cuban mojito. We made stirrers from cut raw sugarcane and lit up rooms with candles in pineapples. Our American friends loved being introduced to these ideas while our Latin friends exposed us to others. We soon started calling our style Latin Chic, which describes the way we live and especially the way we entertain.

Today our parties continue to be well-planned yet easygoing affairs. They're not catered, exhaustive, nor expensive ordeals. Carolina, a television reporter and foodie, is the one in the kitchen, while Isabel, a fashion writer and cocktail aficionada, prepares the mixed drinks and decorates. Together we keep up to the minute with new and old Latin music, making sure our gatherings always have rhythm.

When asked to write a book about Latin Chic we weren't quite sure where to begin, since we have so many ideas, drinks, and recipes. We spent a year whittling down some of our favorite recipes and decor ideas: some new, others traditional. We decided that the best way to share them would be to host ten parties and have them photographed, so you would feel as if you were there with us. While we do most of our entertaining in New York, we used this book as an opportunity to visit friends and celebrate with them in their own cities and countries. From polo players to ballet dancers, from gauchos to Miss Universes, we mingled with Latinos who share our passion for Latin living and entertaining. We introduce you to our friends and include a little on-location history and culture.

In our chapters you will find menus, tips, and ideas from all over Latin America and the Caribbean. After all, the culinary and cultural repertoire of Latin life is vast and varied: There is more to it than tequila shots, tacos, and salsa dancing. It has been influenced by native civilizations such as the Mayans, Aztecs, and Incas, who once occupied much of Central America and South America; by Spanish and Portuguese colonizers; by African slaves brought to the Caribbean and the Americas; and by the numerous ethnic groups—Italians, French, Lebanese, Chinese—who in the late 1800s and throughout the 1900s immigrated to Latin America in search of better social and economic opportunities. So, for this book, we feature drinks, food, and decor reflecting this impressive diversity, like Peruvian ceviche paired with coconut Cuba Libres at our pool party in Puerto Rico. Some of our recipes are extremely traditional, some are updated classics, others are our own inventions, and, of course, there are plenty of family treasures.

For each party, Latin fashion icons working in the United States and Latin America were generous enough to drape us in their gorgeous clothes. These designers, like Carolina Herrera, who had us looking red carpet–worthy for our Oscar party in Los Angeles, continue to stay true to their Latin roots. We are proud to honor their dedication to Latin style.

While this is a party guidebook, you don't have to schedule a party to try a dish from one chapter or an appetizer from another. The menus, which are for two, four, six, eight, and twelve people, can easily be halved or multiplied. As for the drinks, some are meant for pitchers, but there are plenty of recipes for two. Many of the ingredients and decor materials you will need are easy to find at your local grocery, fabric, craft, and hardware stores, but we have provided a source guide to cover the more difficult necessities—like Mexican *lotería* cards or candied guava shells.

Enjoy this book for years to come. It has certainly been an honor and a labor of love to put it together. And while we think it makes for a beautiful book to set on your coffee table, our hope is that you will earmark your favorite pages and even get some of them dirty in the kitchen. As we say in Spanish, *¡Buen provecho!*

Con mucho cariño,

CAROLINA *e* ISABEL

A note from the kitchen: Today most supermarkets sell jalapeños, mangoes, and dulce de leche. Still, there are some Latin ingredients that you may be able to purchase only in specialty stores or online. While we offer substitutions for many, make a note to tell your grocers you want to see essentials like guava paste and coconut water on their shelves. For where to purchase hard-to-find necessities, please see our comprehensive sources on page 225.

LATIN chic

la dulce vida

at vizcaya

A 1950S-INSPIRED CARIBBEAN COCKTAIL PARTY FOR 12

WHEN MY MOTHER DEPARTED HAVANA IN 1960 TO COME TO THE UNITED STATES, SHE ABANDONED MOST OF HER POSSESSIONS,

packing only the barest necessities into the sole suitcase she was allotted. She left behind her fancy dresses to allow space for the one thing that would never go out of style: treasured family photographs.

I've spent hours studying those black-and-white photographs, especially the ones of my beautiful and elegant mamá, from a baby in the 1940s to a sexy babe in the 1950s. My girlfriends could rifle through their American-born parents' attics, playing dress-up in vintage clothes found in trunks, but the photographs were my only visual connection to my mom's—and my—past.

One photograph features my mother at age seventeen, dressed in a scarlet gown made by her *madrina*—her godmother—a form-fitting number embroidered with thousands of crystal beads sewn onto a floor-length satin skirt and topped with a feather headdress. It took her godmother three weeks to make the whole outfit. Mom, one of a hundred guests invited to a costume party that was themed *Piedras Preciosas* ("Precious Jewels"), went as a ruby. In another picture she's at a party in a Havana nightclub, wearing a simple black cocktail dress. Her hair is perfectly coiffed like that of her idol at the time, Gina Lollobrigida.

Inspired by these photos, Carolina and I decided to throw a 1950s Cuban-style party for our friends in Miami, invoking the glamour and sexiness of that era. Looking at old family pictures is a great way to find entertaining ideas. We fawned over the women's Ava Gardner–worthy spaghetti-strap frocks and matching fans. Nipping at their three-inch heels were sexy Latin men, decked out in white dinner jackets or crisp linen guayaberas, mojitos in one hand, cigars in the other. It was these tropical details that would give our cocktail party the feel of that bygone era.

For our celebration, we invited our friends to the fanciest place in Miami: Vizcaya Museum and Gardens, which is legendary for its breathtaking bayside views of Biscayne Bay, Italian Renaissance architecture, and manicured gardens. Completed in 1916 for John Deering, founder of International Harvester, Vizcaya is now open to the public.

We looked to Cuban-American designer Narciso Rodriguez to dress the women in 1950s-inspired dresses. The men were requested to wear button-down shirts or long-sleeved guayaberas. We passed around cigars and paper fans, and served classic Caribbean cocktails and tapas. The party was a success and made for memorable images that, like my mom's photographs, will stand the test of time.

AS THEY ARE FOR MANY CUBANS, minty mojitos are my favorite drink. When they are in season in autumn, I'll add kumquats for color and an additional sweet-and-sour note. Always make each drink individually, as the mashed mint leaves lose their freshness when mojitos are made in large batches. Cut raw sugarcane into thin strips to use as stirrers, adding yet another tropical touch to your party.

4 sprigs mint
2 tablespoons superfine sugar
Juice of 1 lime
2 kumquats, halved
2½ ounces light rum, such as Bacardi Superior
1½ ounces club soda
4 ice cubes
Thinly cut sugarcane

In an old-fashioned glass, lightly mash the mint and sugar for 30 seconds or until the mint aroma is released. Add the lime juice, then squeeze in the kumquats to release their juices into the glass. Drop in some of the kumquat shells, pour in the rum, top with the club soda, give it all a stir, and finish with the ice cubes. Use the sugarcane as a stirrer.

KUMQUAT mojito
SERVES 1

VALENCIA martini

SERVES 2

TRADITIONAL MARTINIS CALL FOR VERMOUTH, but I prefer sherry, which, like vermouth, is a fortified wine. Sherry comes from southern Spain, and in my house, my grandmother would sip chilled fino or manzanilla sherry before dinner. These are the driest types of sherry, so they work well in martinis. Sherry can also be sweet, such as cream and moscatel, which tastes best at room temperature to accompany desserts.

1 ounce dry sherry
4 ounces orange vodka, such as Grey Goose
    L'Orange
1 ounce orange liqueur, such as Cointreau
2 strips orange zest

Combine all the ingredients, except the orange zest, in a cocktail shaker with ice. Shake well and strain into chilled martini glasses. Garnish with orange zest.

MARY pickford

AMERICA'S ORIGINAL SILVER SCREEN SWEETHEART and Hollywood beauty spent time in Cuba, where this pretty pink cocktail was invented in her honor at the bar of the Hotel Sevilla.

5 ounces pineapple juice
4 ounces light rum
2 dashes of grenadine
2 maraschino cherries

Combine the pineapple juice, rum, and grenadine in a cocktail shaker filled with ice. Shake and strain into chilled martini glasses and garnish with maraschino cherries.

CUBA libre

SERVES 1

CUBA LIBRE MEANS "FREE CUBA." Nothing more than rum and Coke mixed together, it was invented in Cuba at the turn of the twentieth century by American soldiers who were there to help win the island's independence from Spain. The American soldiers supplied the Coca-Cola, the Cubans supplied the rum, and the rest is cocktail history. If there's any cut sugarcane leftovers from the mojitos, use them here as stirrers. Also, if you think you are going to be pressed for time, make a pitcher of these just before the party, but don't add the ice until the very last minute.

2 ounces light rum, such as Bacardi Limón
Coca-Cola
Lime wedge
Thinly cut sugarcane

Pour the rum and Coke (about 2 parts Coke to 1 part rum) into a highball glass filled with ice. Squeeze in a lime wedge and stir with a sugarcane.

PRESIDENTE

NOT TO BE CONFUSED WITH THE POPULAR DOMINICAN BEER, the presidente cocktail is a Cuban drink named after General Mario García Menocal, my great-great-grandfather's brother and Cuba's third president. While it's neat to be able to say that a distant relative was a president of a country, I can't say that I know much about him beyond what's in the history books. Family lore has it that he and my great-grandfather had a falling out and rarely spoke. Despite the feud, we love to drink presidentes. Here is my family's recipe, although others I've seen call for sweet vermouth (garnished with maraschino cherries) instead of orange liqueur (garnished with orange slices). Both versions are tasty.

6 ounces light rum
2 ounces dry vermouth
1 ounce orange liqueur, such as Cointreau
Dash of grenadine
2 orange slices

Combine the ingredients in a cocktail shaker filled with ice. Shake and strain into chilled martini glasses. Garnish each glass with an orange slice.

VICTOR's daiquirí

SERVES 2

CAROLINA AND I SPEND QUITE A BIT OF TIME at a Cuban restaurant in midtown Manhattan called Victor's Café, which has been in the city for more than forty years. Originally opened by a Cuban named Victor del Corral, it is now run by his granddaughter, Natalia Zaldivar. Carolina and I have been known to wash down a few of Victor's ham *croquetas* (page 18) with a daiquirí or two. The daiquirí hails from the Cuban mining town of the same name, allegedly invented by an engineer working there in the late 1800s. Hemingway loved to drink daiquirís at Havana's La Floridita bar. He would also drink a version with grapefruit juice, dubbed the Hemingway Special. The frozen daiquirí is a later invention, also created at La Floridita. Victor's recipe is simple and easy to make. Surprise your guests by serving it the original way—in chilled cocktail glasses.

Juice of 2 limes
6 tablespoons superfine sugar
8 ounces light rum, such as Bacardi Superior
2 lime slices

Combine the ingredients, except the lime slices, in a cocktail shaker filled with ice. Shake vigorously and serve in chilled martini glasses. Garnish each glass with a lime slice.

OCTOPUS
JEWEL box salad

FROZEN OR FRESH OCTOPUS has a translucent grayish-blue color that will turn purple and white once cooked. The secret to cooking octopus so that it is tender yet firm is to braise it. I have fond memories of my mother picking out fresh octopus at the fishmonger's and then cutting up the magnificent eight-tentacled creature in our kitchen.

This recipe was inspired by a Lebanese family who lived in our neighborhood in Valencia, Venezuela, where there continues to be a large Lebanese population. They used to make a delicious octopus salad with *granada,* or pomegranate. Today pomegranate molasses is sold in most Middle Eastern markets or in specialty stores (see page 228). The fruit itself, which makes a beautiful garnish, is in season from August to December.

This recipe also calls for Spanish smoked paprika, or *pimentón,* an indispensable ingredient in Spanish cooking. In northern Spain, braised octopus dressed with only smoked paprika and olive oil is also a popular tapas dish.

Spanish paprika is sold in gourmet stores or through online specialty stores. It comes in three varieties: sweet and mild *(dulce),* bittersweet and medium hot *(agridulce),* and hot *(picante).* I like to use either the *agridulce* or the *picante* variety for this dish, though it's a matter of personal taste. A small, 2.5-ounce canister of Spanish paprika will keep for up to two years.

The octopus may be made up to two days ahead, though it should be arranged in the hollowed-out fruit just before serving.

This recipe will fill 6 hollowed-out limes (about 1-ounce portions) and 6 hollowed-out oranges (about 3-ounce portions), for a total of 12 "jewel boxes."

One 6-pound whole frozen (and thawed)
    octopus or two 3-pound octopuses
Olive oil
2 garlic cloves, minced
1 shallot, minced
2 cups white wine
1 bay leaf
3 celery ribs, cut lengthwise and thinly sliced
    crosswise

POMEGRANATE DRESSING

⅓ cup freshly squeezed lime juice
2 tablespoons pomegranate molasses
2 tablespoons extra virgin olive oil
½ teaspoon Spanish smoked paprika
    (*pimentón*)
¼ teaspoon salt, or more to taste
Pinch of sugar
Freshly ground pepper to taste
Seeds from 1 pomegranate (optional),
    for garnish

Cut off the head of the octopus with kitchen scissors and discard. With a paring knife, remove and discard the hard beak inside the mouth of the octopus. Place the octopus in a Dutch oven or other large pot and cover. Turn the heat on low and cook it for about 20 minutes to release any excess water. Remove the pan from the heat, discard all excess water, and place the octopus on a plate.

Coat the bottom of a Dutch oven with olive oil. Over medium heat, sauté the garlic and shallot until they soften, a couple of minutes. Return the octopus to the pot and fill it with an inch of white wine, about 2 cups. Add the bay leaf, cover, and braise over low-medium heat for about 1½ hours (the liquid should bubble gently), or until the thickest part is tender enough so that a knife tip pierces through with little resistance. Discard the bay leaf.

Remove the octopus from the heat, drain, and cool. Carefully discard any loose membranes clinging to its tentacles, but do not remove the suction cups. Cut the tentacles into small pieces, 1 to 3 inches in length, and place them in a medium bowl with the celery slices. Cover with plastic wrap and refrigerate for at least an hour.

In a small bowl mix all of the dressing ingredients with a whisk or fork. Toss the octopus and celery with the dressing and refrigerate until ready to serve. Adjust the salt to taste. Serve the salad chilled and garnished with pomegranate seeds, if desired.

Diablitos a Caballo

MALBEC prunes

I MUST CREDIT ANA MARÍA ALVARO, a Chilean friend who hosts grand cocktail parties in Miami, for sharing this easy and tasty *pasa palo*, which is what we call hors d'oeuvres in Venezuela. While researching recipes for this book, I learned that Aussies and Brits also serve prunes wrapped in bacon. They call them "devils on horseback," a cute moniker that in Spanish translates to *diablitos a caballo*.

This recipe will make about 40 prunes.

2 pieces star anise
1 cup red wine, preferably Malbec
One 12-ounce bag pitted prunes (about 40)
5 ounces dried papaya, cut into forty ¼-inch
    by ½-inch matchstick pieces
20 bacon slices, halved

Soak 40 toothpicks in water for at least 20 minutes, then pat them dry.

In a bowl large enough to hold the prunes, steep the anise in the wine.

Preheat the oven to 350°F. Line a large sheet pan with aluminum foil. With a paring knife, make a small incision at one end of each prune and stuff each prune with a piece of papaya. Soak the prunes in the wine for about an hour, then drain.

Wrap a bacon slice around each stuffed prune and secure with a toothpick. Place the prunes on the prepared sheet pan and bake, turning the prunes halfway through, for 15 to 18 minutes, or until the bacon is crisp. Serve warm.

TOSTONES

THE FIRST TIME I MET ISABEL'S MOM, Sara, she made a plate of these crunchy, twice-fried plantain rounds and told me how these were a top-seller when she owned Sarita's, a Cuban restaurant in Atlanta. In Colombia and Panama they are called *patacones*.

Plantains are omnipresent in Latin America, where they are also used to make soft empanadas and mofongo (page 84), or sliced thin, fried, and sold in bags like potato chips. They can be found in the produce section of most supermarkets. For this recipe, use green (unripe) plantains with no signs of yellowing.

Tostones may be made up to a couple of hours ahead, left covered at room temperature, and then reheated in a 300°F oven until warm.

This makes about 28 tostones.

4 large green plantains
Vegetable or canola oil for deep-frying
Salt

Trim the plantain ends. Slice the plantains into 1 to 1½-inch circles. With a paring knife, cut and peel off the tough skins. Heat enough oil over moderate heat in a frying pan to cover the plantains. When hot (about 350°F on a frying thermometer), fry the plantains in batches—without crowding the pan—until slightly tender and golden on each side, 5 to 7 minutes per batch.

Remove the plantains and put on a plate lined with paper towels. While they're still hot, place another paper towel on top and flatten each plantain by pressing it with a large wooden spoon.

Refry the flattened plantains in sizzling oil (375°F) for about a minute, and return to a plate newly lined with paper towels. Sprinkle with salt and serve warm.

SHREDDED BEEF WITH CAYENNE-KICKIN' SWEET-potato puree

W HEN I WAS A KID, *carne mechada* was one of my favorite meals: spooned over rice or stuffed in *arepas* (page 194). Though *carne mechada* is a traditional Venezuela beef dish, it is eaten in many Latin countries and called by different names. In Cuba it's known as *ropa vieja,* which means "old clothes."

We decided to serve this hearty, moist meat dish in vintage martini glasses purchased at a flea market. We piped a side of bright orange sweet-potato puree as an accompaniment.

The beef's flavorful base is made by sautéing chopped onions, garlic, and peppers. This classic Caribbean base is known as a *sofrito* and is also used to flavor chicken, pork, fish, and rice dishes. Both the meat and sweet-potato puree in this recipe may be made up to a day ahead and warmed on the stovetop before being arranged in the martini glasses.

Depending on the size of the martini glasses, this recipe will yield 12 to 14 servings. To serve traditionally, with a side of white rice, there's enough here for 6 entrée-sized portions.

2½ pounds flank steak
2 large Spanish onions, 1 cut into quarters,
    1 coarsely chopped
2 celery stalks, with leaves
1 bay leaf
1 teaspoon black peppercorns
Salt
3 tablespoons unsalted butter
¼ cup olive oil
8 garlic cloves, minced
3 bell peppers (green, red, and yellow),
    sliced in long, thin strips
½ cup white wine or dry sherry
½ cup raisins
½ cup pitted manzanilla olives
    (with or without pimientos), chopped
3 ounces tomato paste
1½ teaspoons cumin
1 tablespoon dried Mexican oregano
Freshly ground black pepper

Using a knife or kitchen scissors, cut the flank steak across the grain into approximately three pieces, 3 to 4 inches long. In a stockpot, combine the steak, roughly 2½ cups of cold water, the quartered onion, celery, bay leaf, and peppercorns. Bring to a boil. Add a palmful of salt and simmer uncovered for 1½ hours, occasionally skimming any impurities (foam) off the top.

Remove the cooked meat and set aside. Strain the broth and reserve 1 cup. Once the meat is cool enough to handle, shred it finely with your hands or a fork.

In a large skillet, heat the butter and olive oil. Add the garlic and shredded beef, sautéing over medium-high heat until the thin beef pieces start to lightly sear, 5 to 10 minutes. Adjust the heat to medium-low and add the chopped onion and peppers, sautéing until softened. Pour in the wine and the reserved broth, and simmer. Stir in the raisins, olives, tomato paste, cumin, and oregano, mixing well. Season with salt and pepper to taste. Continue to cook over low heat, partially covered, for at least an hour, stirring intermittently, until the liquid has reduced by at least half and the meat is tender.

When ready to serve, fill a martini glass with the beef and, using a pastry bag or a large spoon, add a side of sweet-potato puree (recipe follows).

cayenne-kickin' sweet-potato puree

THE SWEET POTATO, ORIGINALLY FROM THE AMERICAS, is botanically unrelated to the potato. In North America, the most common variety is known as the Louisiana yam, with brown skin and orange flesh. There is also a white sweet potato with pink skin called the *boniato,* which is extremely popular in South America but not always readily available in the States. Either sweet potato variety may be used in this recipe.

When adding cayenne, remember—a little goes a long way.

This recipe will make fill 12 to 14 martini glasses or make 6 side portions.

5 to 6 medium sweet potatoes
4 tablespoons unsalted butter
½ cup, or slightly more, heavy cream
Pinch of salt
¼ teaspoon grated nutmeg
Pinch of cayenne pepper, or more to taste
Salt and freshly ground black pepper

Wash and cut the sweet potatoes in three to four pieces. Place them in a pot with enough water to cover and bring to a boil. Cook until you can easily push a knife through the thickest parts, about 20 minutes.

Drain, cool, and peel the skins off. Cut into smaller pieces.

In a medium saucepan melt the butter over low heat. Add the sweet potatoes and coat with the butter. Add the cream, salt, and nutmeg, and cook until small bubbles form on the sides of the pot (a sign that the boiling point is around the corner).

Remove from the heat. Using a handheld immersion blender or food processor, puree until smooth. Mix in the cayenne to taste. Season with salt and pepper to taste.

THESE BITE-SIZED *PASA PALOS* TAKE ONLY MINUTES TO PREP AND BAKE. They are made with Manchego cheese, which gets its name from La Mancha, a region in the center of Spain, where the cheese has traditionally been produced using the milk of a breed of sheep called Manchega. Manchego has a semifirm or firm texture, depending on how long it has been aged, and a translucent dark brown rind.

As for the mushrooms, select the largest mushrooms you can find. Look for ones that aren't bruised and that have stems tightly attached to the caps.

These mushrooms may be prepped up to a day ahead, refrigerated, and baked just minutes before serving.

This makes 32 stuffed mushrooms.

32 cremini or white button mushrooms
1 tablespoon unsalted butter
1 shallot, minced
Salt and freshly ground black pepper
⅛ teaspoon grated nutmeg
6 ounces Manchego, coarsely grated
¼ cup (preferably fresh) breadcrumbs

mushrooms stuffed with manchego cheese

Wipe the mushrooms clean with a damp towel; do not rinse them unless they're extremely dirty. Trim and discard the very bottoms of the stems, about ¼ inch. Gently detach the remaining stems from the caps and finely chop these.

Preheat the oven to 350°F.

In a saucepan over low-medium heat, melt the butter, add the chopped mushroom stems with the shallot, and sauté until the shallot is translucent and the mixture is dry, 7 to 8 minutes. Add the salt, pepper, and nutmeg to taste. Allow the mushroom mixture to cool.

In a small bowl, combine the mushroom-shallot mixture with the grated Manchego and breadcrumbs. Generously fill each mushroom cap with the mixture. Place the stuffed mushrooms on a baking sheet and bake until the cheese has melted and the tops are lightly golden, 10 to 15 minutes. Serve warm.

CROQUETAS WERE A WAY FOR COOKS to use up leftover meat, chicken, or fish. Leftovers were ground up, mixed with a béchamel sauce, breaded, and fried.

This *croqueta* recipe is adapted from the one used at Victor's Café in New York and calls for both cooked and smoked ham. When Isabel and I worked as reporters for Time Inc., we would meet for lunch at this Latin hangout. In fact, we started plotting this book over platefuls of ham croquettes and Cuban coffee.

The *croqueta* dough can be made up to two days ahead. The *croquetas* themselves may be fried earlier in the day and served at room temperature or warmed in a 300°F oven. They are also great over mixed greens.

This recipe will make approximately 25 croquetas.

½ pound cooked deli ham, sliced
¼ pound smoked deli ham, sliced
1 tablespoon vegetable oil
1 tablespoon butter
¼ cup minced white onion (about half a medium onion)
1 tablespoon minced jalapeño (no seeds; about ½ jalapeño)
½ cup flour
⅔ cup whole milk
2 tablespoons finely chopped parsley
Vegetable or canola oil for frying
3 large eggs
2 cups breadcrumbs (fresh or dried)

VICTOR's ham croquetas

In a food processor, pulse the ham slices for about 20 seconds, until ground into very small pieces. Set aside.

Heat the oil in a skillet over medium heat. Add the butter and sauté the onion and jalapeño until soft, about 4 minutes. Reduce the heat to low and add the flour, stirring rapidly with a wooden spoon until a thick paste forms. Add the milk, continue to stir, keeping the heat low enough so that it does not boil. After 1 minute, add the chopped ham and parsley, turn off the heat, and continue stirring on the stovetop until the *croqueta* dough is well mixed.

Place the dough in a bowl to cool. Then cover and chill in the refrigerator for at least 3 hours or overnight.

Once the dough has chilled, shape about 1½ tablespoons into 3-inch cylinders, the size of a lipstick tube.

In a large skillet, heat ½ inch to 1 inch oil to 375°F.

Clear off enough counter space to set up an assembly line with plates filled with uncooked shaped *croquetas,* a bowl with the 3 whisked eggs, another with the breadcrumbs, and a couple of extra plates lined with paper towels for the fried *croquetas.*

Lightly coat the *croquetas* in the egg, dredge in the breadcrumbs, and fry them in batches without crowding the pan. Turn them occasionally to promote even browning.

Once they're golden brown, about 3 to 5 minutes, remove them with a slotted spoon to the paper towel-lined plates.

Cascos de Guayaba con Queso de Cabra

PRESERVED
GUAVA shells with
goat cheese

Our grandmothers and mothers feasted on preserved guava and cheese, and we follow in their tradition. My maternal grandmother liked to pair local Venezuelan farmstead cheese with her fuchsia-colored guava shells, while Isabel's maternal grandmother was partial to cream cheese. For our party, we decided to top this Caribbean sweet with fresh goat cheese.

Buy canned guava shells packed in a syrup, preferably the pink Caribbean guavas (see page 228). Asian canned guavas, which are cream-colored and not as sweet, may be used as a substitute.

This will make 12 stuffed shells.

12 ounces fresh goat cheese,
    such as Montrachet or Bûcheron
One 16-ounce can preserved guava shells
    (about 12 preserved guava shells), chilled

Spoon a heaping tablespoon of the goat cheese inside each chilled guava shell. Serve immediately on small plates, such as espresso plates.

language of the fan

While fans make inexpensive party favors and beautiful gifts, they were traditionally used for battling tropical temperatures, swatting mosquitoes, and even mild flirting. One of my great-aunts taught me that fans—and how they are held—have a language all their own.

Fan drawn down right cheek	I love you
Fan drawn down left cheek	I don't like you
Fan held open across the face	Follow me
Fan drawn across the eyes	I am sorry
Shooing motion	Scram, kiddo

cigar smoking 101

In Cuba, men dip the caps (the side you inhale from) of their cigars into small shots of Cuban coffee (espresso with extra sugar) before taking a puff. The coffee sweetens the tobacco flavor. Some women also smoke cigars or cigarillos, which are thin cigars. Here are a few other tips I learned from my grandfather who smoked a cigar a day until he passed away at eighty-nine.

- Don't cut the whole cap off or the tobacco wrapper will come undone. You want to just snip it. There needs to be some roundness left in the cap.
- Don't tap your cigar ash. The ash should never be longer than a thimble and should come off naturally when you rest it in the ashtray.
- Don't relight a cigar after an hour or two, max, or it will taste stale.
- Refrain from extinguishing cigars in plants or half-empty glasses; the smell quickly goes from tolerable to vile.

praising papa

Channel Ernest at your event, but not with a Hemingway look-alike contest. Honor the writer whose home in Cuba, La Finca Vigía, was a setting for creative inspiration. Visit a used-book store and buy some vintage Hemingway hardcover books. Stack them and distribute them on tables or wrap with raffia and give as party favors. This is an easy and inexpensive decor idea for other parties, too. Old books—even campy paperback books from the 1960s and 1970s—add a lot of charm.

guayaberas

Popular in the Caribbean and Mexico, with purported origins in Cuba, these traditionally long-sleeved, 100-percent linen men's shirts accented with multiple pockets and pintucks enabled stylish men to lounge elegantly yet comfortably at fancy affairs. You can have an authentic one made by the king, Ramón Puig, at his world-famous La Casa de Las Guayaberas in Miami's Little Havana. Puig, a tailor from Cuba, has been fashioning these shirts for more than sixty years. His clients include Hollywood stars, royalty, and U.S. presidents. If Miami is out of the question, you can get them online and also at such stores as Bloomingdale's, Dillard's, Macy's, and JCPenney, where long- and short-sleeved versions are popping up in men's departments everywhere. Perry Ellis International, which is a Cuban-American-owned company, makes lightweight and tropically designed guayaberas, and sells them under the Cubavera and Havanera lines.

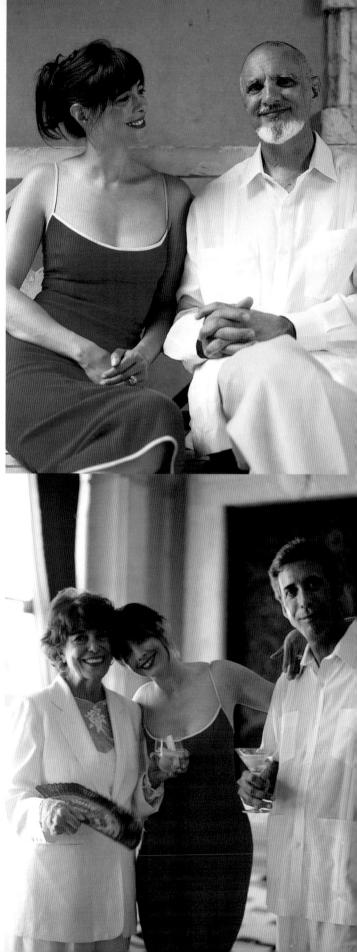

light my way

Forgo candles and add touches of warm light to enchanted evenings with large, bright paper lanterns that guests can carry to illuminate dark pathways. They are inexpensive and easily available online and at party, craft, and dollar stores.

flights of fancy

Canaries, parakeets, and parrots decorate our tropical past; my grandmother always doted on her fine yellow-feathered friend, Tom Jones. Carolina's uncle Jordi had an ornery pet green macaw named Pepito. This little guy goes by the name of B.

citrus jewel boxes

Hollow out lime, lemon, and oranges, and use them as mini-tapas bowls for octopus salad or your own recipes. They make a beautiful—and simple—presentation. Using a paring knife, cut ¼ from the top. Then carefully run the paring knife along the inside to release the pulp. Using a spoon, hollow out the fruit.

BEATS

There's a popular expression in Cuba, *moliendo café,* which means "grinding coffee," but it's also used to describe dances that "press the flesh," like boleros and sons. Music is always present in Cuban life, and its Afro-Cuban rhythms are the backbone of any good Caribbean party. My mom tells me that at the parties she went to, there were always one or two live bands. Our budget didn't allow for that extravagance, so Carolina's brother Christian serenaded the crowd with his classical guitar. There's nothing like live music to add atmosphere, but if you don't have luck finding a crowd crooner, here are five CDs for dancing and *moliendo café,* with rhythmic hip-shaking rumba, mambo, salsa, bolero, and even a little Spanish flamenco and Cuban jazz thrown in for good measure.

Lo Mejor de lo Mejor   Beny Moré
100% Azúcar: The Best of Celia Cruz con La Sonora Matancera
Buena Vista Social Club Presents Ibrahim Ferrer
Lágrimas Negras   Diego El Cigala and Bebo Valdés
No Limit: Afro-Cuban Jazz   Roberto Fonseca

latina ladies

who lunch

A HEALTHY VEGETARIAN MENU FOR 6

IN THE SUMMER OF 1980, MY FATHER, A UNIVERSITY PROFESSOR IN VENEZUELA, WAS ACCEPTED INTO A PH.D. PROGRAM IN THE UNITED STATES. WITH SHEETS EXPERTLY TUCKED INTO THE MATTRESSES, TOYS and books left undisturbed on their shelves, and the front door double-bolted, we left our apartment in Valencia and boarded a PanAm flight to Miami International Airport.

In elementary school I learned English, how to play dodge ball, and how to make Rice Krispy treats. At home my parents spoke Spanish, read the Venezuelan dailies, and played the folkloric *joropos* of Simon Díaz. For show-and-tell I brought in Venezuelan toys like *perinolas* and a *quarto* (four-string guitar). My class was patient with my English, and my friends invited me to their homes for Thanksgiving and taught me the rules of American football. I shared with them pictures of family vacations on the turquoise beaches of Morrocoy and the snowy peaks of the Andes. I told tales of my uncle's green talking parrot named Pepito, who could rattle off names and phrases.

Though I was born in Venezuela, I spent most of my childhood in Miami. It's a city that has gone through many changes. As I became more American, Miami became more Latin. Today Spanish is its unofficial language, backyards teem with wild mangroves, iguanas, and papaya trees, and you can choose between a Venezuelan, Chilean, or Argentine *empanada* for breakfast.

At eighteen, I left Miami to study in North Carolina. After a stay there, I lived briefly in California and then settled in New York City. But Miami is still home. It's a place that, like me, has two backgrounds: one Latin, one American. My parents and many friends who knew me as a girl still live there. I drive through familiar streets, past my first school and our first house. I slip into the warm waters of South Beach, stay out late dancing salsa in Coconut Grove, and hear Spanish—spoken with all different accents—while enjoying a plate of *empanadas*.

For this chapter, Isabel and I wanted to celebrate the Latin cultural diversity that is Miami. We invited new and old friends for a relaxing afternoon of card playing and conversation. A light vegetarian menu complemented a bevy of nonalcoholic drinks. Fashion model Leticia Grendene, born to Mexican and Puerto Rican parents, opened up her Miami home to us. Alessandra, her lovely five-year-old daughter, set the table using her starfish collection as napkin holders.

After lunch we lounged by the pool, sipped fresh fruit juices, and played games with Spanish *barajas* (cards). Dayanara Torres, a former Miss Universe and now a television actress, taught us *brisca,* which she grew up playing in her native Puerto Rico. Having settled in Miami, she and her sister—both expert *brisca* players—shamelessly beat the rest of us every time. We took it all in stride as we basked in the sunlight of a perfect South Florida afternoon.

THIS IS THE RECIPE OF NEW YORK CHEF AARON SANCHEZ. Carolina and I are fans of his restaurant, Paladar, in lower Manhattan, where we often go for pan-Latin cooking. This simple thirst-quencher is popular for breakfast in Mexico and Central America, and also thought to be a cure for hangovers. In Venezuela and Colombia they call it *chicha*. In Central American countries, like Costa Rica, they make it with corn. In Bolivia they make it with peanuts. It's a sweet drink that looks milky but is entirely dairy-free. I like to drink it with a scoop of chocolate ice cream for dessert. This treat is called a Cubanito.

2 cups plain white rice
4 cinnamon sticks
1 cup sugar

In a large bowl (or two smaller bowls) soak the rice and cinnamon sticks in 2 quarts of water overnight. The rice will soak up some of the water and become soft. Remove the cinnamon sticks and puree the rice mixture in a blender, in 2 batches for 2 minutes each. Put the pureed rice in a saucepan with the sugar and 2 quarts of water. Simmer over low heat for 20 minutes. Do not stir. You want all the liquid to rise to the top of the pan and the rice, which will congeal, to stay at the bottom of the pan. Pour the rice water through a fine-mesh sieve lined with cheesecloth or a clean tea towel; twist the cloth to squeeze out all the liquid and discard any of the rice solids. Pour the liquid, which will be white, into a pitcher, and chill in the refrigerator. Serve over ice.

HORCHATA de arroz

SERVES 8

AGUA de sapo

DON'T BE PUT OFF BY THE NAME—this isn't a witchy amphibian brew. *Agua de sapo* is a delicious citrus-ginger drink. It's popular in the Limón region of Costa Rica, where the culture and food have African and Caribbean roots. Inhabitants along the bucolic Caribbean coast cool off with variations on this healthy drink, the main ingredients being ginger, lemon or lime juice, and molasses. For simplicity's sake, we substitute sugar for the molasses. Honey is a tasty option, too.

3-inch piece of ginger root, peeled and
    roughly chopped
⅓ cup sugar
Juice of 2 lemons
6 lemon wedges

Put the ginger in a pan with 6 cups cold water. Cover the pan and bring to a boil. Reduce heat to low and simmer for 10 minutes. Remove the pan from the heat and cool. Discard the ginger pieces and stir in the sugar until it dissolves. Pour the liquid into a pitcher and refrigerate. Once cold, stir in the juice of two lemons. Pour the *agua de sapo* into glasses over ice and garnish with the lemon wedges.

VIRGIN mojito

SERVES 1

HERE'S A DRINK WITH THE FLAVOR OF A MOJITO BUT WITHOUT THE PUNCH. My mom would make me this drink when I was a kid, at parties, when all the adults were drinking the real thing. It calls for an extra sour note, so add more sugar if need be.

4 sprigs mint
1 tablespoon superfine sugar
Juice of 1 lime, plus wedges
Juice of 1 lemon, plus wedges
Club soda

In an old-fashioned glass, mash the mint and sugar. Add the lime and lemon juices along with a few lemon and lime wedges. Fill the glass with ice and top with the club soda.

GUAVA cooler

serves 8

SOME PEOPLE FIND PLAIN GUAVA JUICE TOO FILLING. Cranberry juice, a very North American ingredient, dilutes its richness without compromising the sweet flavor. If you want some fizz, top the pitcher with Sprite or 7UP.

4 cups cranberry juice
4 cups guava juice

Mix the juices in a pitcher. Serve over ice.

CILANTRO soup

THIS CREAMY SOUP—GARNISHED WITH ALMONDS—is a popular Mexican starter. The first time I tried it was on a trip to Puerto Vallarta. My friends and I stopped at an off-the-beaten-path restaurant for lunch, and afterward I went into the kitchen to meet the chef—a seventy-year-old grandmother—and ask for her recipe.

Cilantro is commonly associated with Latin American and Thai dishes, but it was also popular in ancient Roman cuisine. It's found year-round in most grocery stores and generally sold in bunches. Look for bright green leaves with no signs of wilting. To store cilantro in your refrigerator for up to five days, place the bunch, stems down, in a glass of water and cover with a plastic bag secured with a rubber band. Make sure to change the water every couple of days. This soup may be made a day ahead and served either hot or cold.

This recipe serves 6 to 8.

4½ tablespoons unsalted butter
4 garlic cloves, roughly chopped
1 medium onion, coarsely chopped
3 small potatoes, peeled and cubed
2 small parsnips, sliced
6 celery stalks with leaves, coarsely chopped
6 cups low-sodium vegetable stock
1 cup fresh cilantro (leaves and stems)
½ cup heavy cream or plain yogurt
Salt and freshly ground black pepper to taste
3 tablespoons dry sherry
2 handfuls of blanched almonds,
    coarsely chopped, for garnish

Melt the butter in a medium pan. Over low heat, sauté the garlic and onion until the onion is soft. Add the potatoes, parsnips, celery, stock, and cilantro. Simmer over low heat until the potatoes and parsnips are cooked through, about 25 minutes.

When slightly cooled, puree the soup in a blender or food processor (you will probably need to do this in a couple of batches). You may also use a handheld immersion blender. Return the soup to the pan and stir in the cream and the salt and pepper. Warm over low heat, but do not bring to a boil. Remove from the heat and stir in the sherry. Garnish with the almonds just before serving.

AVOCADO butter

MANTEQUILLA DE LOS POBRES, "POOR MEN'S BUTTER," is how Chileans refer to this healthy spread. Long before the arrival of the Europeans, avocados were being cultivated from Peru to the Rio Grande. In fact, the word "avocado" comes from the Aztec word *ahuacatl*.

You can use either Hass or Florida avocados. Hass are the smaller of the two and have pebbly, purplish-black skin. Florida avocados have smooth, bright green skin and a fruitier taste. Look for ripe avocados that yield slightly to pressure; avoid any with bruises.

This butter will last up to a couple of days, covered, in the refrigerator. The lime juice prevents it from turning brown. It's a delightful spread on Cuban crackers, toasted Cuban bread, or French baguettes.

This recipe makes about 2 cups.

2 Hass avocados or 1 large Florida avocado
⅓ cup freshly squeezed lime juice
    (juice of about 2 limes)
⅓ cup extra virgin olive oil
½ teaspoon sugar
½ teaspoon fresh tarragon leaves
Salt and freshly ground black pepper to taste

Slice the avocados and place them in a food processor. Add the rest of the ingredients and pulse until smooth and buttery. Refrigerate.

HANDLING AN AVOCADO

To cut open an avocado, use a sharp knife and cut around the pit lengthwise. With your hands, rotate and separate the two halves. Stick a knife into the pit, twist, and remove. Using a spoon, scoop the avocado meat away from the skin.

NOTHING ANNOUNCES THE ARRIVAL OF SUMMER LIKE A RIPE TOMATO SALAD. This recipe comes our way through Sergio Sigala, executive chef for South Beach's Casa Tua restaurant, which is owned by Leticia Grendene and her husband, Miky.

Sergio's salad, best in summer when luscious tomatoes are in season, features all different types of tomatoes: heirloom, pear, cherry, and tomatillo. Tomatillos have a papery husk, which must be removed. They're available in some supermarkets and most Latin food stores.

The dressing may be made up to one week ahead and stored in the refrigerator. It may also be used as a marinade for grilled eggplant, chicken, or fish.

The salad serves 6.

TOMATILLO DRESSING

YIELDS ABOUT 2½ CUPS

8 ounces tomatillos (about 4 large tomatillos), husks removed
1 tablespoon minced shallot
1¼ cups olive oil
10 basil leaves
1 teaspoon sugar
½ teaspoon hot pepper sauce, such as Tabasco
½ to 1 teaspoon salt
⅓ cup lime juice (about 4 limes)

HEIRLOOM TOMATO salad with tomatillo dressing

Soak the husked tomatillos in a bowl of warm water for 20 minutes to remove their sticky resin. Place all the ingredients in a food processor and process until smooth. Refrigerate until ready to use.

HEIRLOOM TOMATO SALAD

Extra virgin olive oil
1 cup pine nuts
1 teaspoon cumin
1 poblano pepper, cored, seeded, and roasted
½ red onion, thinly sliced
2 pounds mixed tomatoes
1 mango
Handful of parsley leaves
Handful of cilantro leaves
Handful of basil leaves

In a skillet add a tablespoon of olive oil and toast the pine nuts over high heat, shaking the pan a few times. As soon as the pine nuts begin to turn a golden color, stir in the cumin and remove the pan from the heat.

Roast the poblano pepper (see below). Soak the onion slices in a bowl with enough cold water to cover, for 10 minutes, dry, and set aside. Cut the tomatoes into different shapes. Peel and shave the mango into long, flat strips, using a vegetable peeler. With a knife, slice the roasted poblano pepper into strips, called *rajas*. Arrange all the salad ingredients, including the herbs, on individual plates and drizzle enough dressing to taste. Serve immediately.

ROASTING PEPPERS

To roast peppers on a gas stovetop, turn the flame wide open, place the peppers directly in the fire, and rotate them as they begin to char. If you don't have a gas range, you can roast them in a 375°F–400°F oven, turning them a few times, until the skin chars completely.

Next, place the peppers inside a bowl covered with plastic wrap. When cool, remove the charred skin with your hands over a bowl so as not to lose their juices.

I CAME UP WITH THIS RECIPE ONE DAY WHEN ANABELLE DE GALE, my best friend from the sixth grade, and her fiancé came to New York for a visit. Anabelle's a vegetarian, and I wanted to impress her with a beautiful and tasty entrée. It was such a hit that Isabel and I now serve it at our parties.

The aromatic black bean filling complements the hot sauce, a staple condiment on the tables of Spain's Canary Islands. The hot sauce is best made at least a day ahead, and it can be kept refrigerated for up to three weeks—just stir well before using. It's also good with grilled zucchini or broiled salmon.

The crepes may be put together hours ahead and baked at the last minute.

This recipe makes 12 to 16 crepes.

CARIBBEAN CREPES WITH canary islands hot sauce

CREPE BATTER

4 large eggs
1 cup all-purpose flour
1 cup milk, preferably whole
½ tablespoon ground allspice
½ tablespoon salt
Pinch of sugar
4 tablespoons butter, softened,
    and extra butter for cooking crepes

Olive oil

½ medium Spanish onion, finely chopped
   (about 1 cup)

½ celery rib, cut crosswise, then thinly sliced

½ cup dry sherry

1 bay leaf

1 tablespoon plus 1 teaspoon cumin

1 tablespoon sugar

One 15.5-ounce can black beans,
   drained and rinsed

Salt and freshly ground black pepper to taste

9 ounces Oaxaca or fresh mozzarella cheese,
   shredded coarsely

2 large orange peppers, roasted
   (see page 41), cut into ¼-inch-long slivers

In a small bowl, beat the eggs and set aside. Sift the flour into a medium bowl and whisk in the milk until smooth. Add the eggs, allspice, salt, sugar, and butter. Continue to whisk until there are no lumps. Let the batter rest at room temperature for at least 20 minutes.

Lightly coat a medium saucepan with olive oil, and heat. Sauté the onion and celery over medium heat. When the onion is tender, lower the heat, pour the sherry into the pan, and reduce for a couple of minutes. Add the bay leaf, cumin, sugar, and 2 to 3 tablespoons water. Stir. Add the beans, stirring gently so they don't break up too much.

After a couple of minutes, cover, and lower the heat. Simmer for 10 to 15 minutes, adding more water if necessary so there is enough liquid to keep the beans moist. The beans should have a bit of juice, but they should not be soupy.

Remove from the heat. Add salt and pepper to taste.

Coat a glass or ceramic baking dish (large enough to fit the rolled-up crepes) with butter or olive oil. Preheat the oven to 350°F.

Heat a crepe pan (8 to 9 inches) or other nonstick pan over low-to-medium heat. When the pan is hot, pour in about ¼ cup batter at a time. Working quickly, lift the pan, swirl the batter around to form an even, thin crepe (remove any excess batter or drizzle more to cover up any holes), and return to the stovetop.

The cooking time for crepes should be no longer than 30 seconds to a minute per side. Once one side is cooked, give the pan a shake; if the crepe moves easily and if the bottom is a light tan color, flip and cook the other side for 15 to 30 seconds. Stack the crepes on a plate.

Fill each crepe (using the less attractive side) with roughly 2 tablespoons black beans, 2 tablespoons shredded cheese, and 2 to 3 slivers of roasted peppers. Roll them up like big cigars and place them side by side in a prepared baking dish. Sprinkle the remaining cheese on top. Bake for about 10 minutes in a preheated oven.

Top with Canary Islands Hot Sauce or serve the sauce on the side.

canary islands hot sauce

ABOUT 2 CUPS

3 large garlic cloves, peeled and halved
1 small to medium red bell pepper, cored,
    seeded, and quartered
2 fingerling red peppers (also called
    cayenne peppers) with seeds, cored
One 2- to 3-inch slice of day-old baguette,
    quartered
Extra virgin olive oil, about ½ cup
Pinch of sugar
Salt and freshly ground black pepper to taste

In a food processor combine the first four ingredients. Pulse until the bread, garlic, and peppers have a crumbly texture. While the food processor is running, drizzle in the olive oil and process until smooth. Add the sugar and salt and pepper. Refrigerate until ready to use.

Before serving, let it come to room temperature for at least 10 minutes, and stir.

MY PATERNAL GRANDMOTHER, *NONNA*, is a world traveler and a fine home cook who moved to Venezuela in the 1950s after living in both Italy and Eritrea. She settled in the Andean town of Mérida and then moved to Valencia. She always said, "I've lived my life with a suitcase in front of me." Her husband, my *Nonno,* was often away on business, and so my *Nonna* found solace in the kitchen.

This is a simple fruit dessert *Nonna* still makes with fresh berries and Caribbean fruits such as mango and guanabana, also known as soursop. Feel free to substitute other seasonal berries.

The sugar and wine draw out the flavors of the fruits to create a sweet, drinkable ambrosia.

The salad may be made up to a day ahead, then covered and refrigerated. The cream should be whipped right before serving.

This serves 6 to 8.

1 cup blackberries
1 cup raspberries or blueberries
1 cup hulled and halved strawberries
1 cup cubed mango or guanabana
½ cup red wine, such as Cabernet
¼ cup sugar (more or less, depending on the sweetness of the fruit), plus 3 tablespoons sugar
2 teaspoons fresh, finely chopped tarragon leaves
½ pint heavy (or light) cream

MACERATED FRUITS AND BERRIES WITH TARRAGON AND fresh cream

Combine the 4 cups of fruit in a glass bowl. Pour in the wine, sprinkle with the ¼ cup sugar, and gently toss. Cover and chill for at least an hour.

When ready to serve, whip the cream and 3 tablespoons sugar by hand or in a mixer, until soft and fluffy. Serve the fruit in small soup or ice-cream bowls, with a dollop of cream on top.

DULCE de leche

WHEN I FIRST SAW THAT DULCE DE LECHE HAD BECOME AN ICE-CREAM FLAVOR, I thought to myself, "Latin food has arrived!" I grew up eating dulce de leche on crackers, cookies, toast, and in cakes. It is a traditional Latin sweet that—while sold in many grocery stores—is easy to make at home.

Dulce de leche roughly translates into "milk jam." Argentines claim it as their own confection, though in Colombia they call it *arequipe,* and in Mexico they call it *cajeta.* Mexicans usually make their version from goat's milk, which undercuts the sweetness with a slight tang. In Mexico, pastry shops sell *churros,* long cylinders of fried dough filled with *cajeta* and sprinkled with sugar.

This recipe will make about 3 cups.

Three 14-ounce cans sweetened
  condensed milk

Preheat the oven to 425°F.

Pour the condensed milk into a cake pan and cover with aluminum foil. Place in a roasting pan filled with enough water so that the bottom half of the cake pan is surrounded by water. This cooking method is called *baño maria,* or "water bath."

Place in the preheated oven for 1 hour and 45 minutes. Remove and let cool. Transfer to a container, stir, cover, and refrigerate.

MONTSE'S
GREEN mango jam

WHENEVER I WOULD COME HOME FROM COLLEGE, Mom and I would make all kinds of preserves with fruits from our backyard. We'd wake up early in the morning while the rest of the house was still asleep.

This mango jam, named after my mother, is a thick spread that we use on toast or with mozzarella, goat cheese, or Brie.

Select very green mangoes with little or no sign of a ripening red color, and make sure they are firm.

If you don't want to weigh out the proportions, here is a cheat sheet: 3 pounds whole green mangoes will call for approximately 3 cups sugar and 1 tablespoon lemon juice.

Green mangoes
Sugar
Lemon or lime juice

Place as many green mangoes as you want in a large stockpot and fill with enough water to cover. Bring to a boil. Boil the mangoes for 30 minutes. They should feel bloated and yield to pressure. Drain the water and set the mangoes aside.

When cool enough to handle, peel off the skins and then, using a knife and your hands, remove as much of the pulp as you can into a bowl. Weigh and write down the amount of pulp you've extracted. In a food processor or blender, pulse the mango pulp for about a minute, until smooth.

Measure out two-thirds of the pulp's weight in sugar. Place the pulp and sugar in a saucepan and simmer on low, stirring occasionally with a wooden spoon. Stir in approximately 1 tablespoon lemon juice for every 3 cups sugar. Cook, uncovered, for 30 minutes. Let cool and then refrigerate until ready to use.

maritime treasures

Gifts from the sea perked up our picnic. Large starfish kept the napkins from blowing away, and a vase full of light-colored shells worked as a stylish centerpiece. If you can't find what you need dotting the seashore, pick up shells at a craft store or beachside tourist shop.

take-home treat

We divided Carolina's extra avocado butter into small ramekins and covered them with plastic wrap and cloth cut from a fabric remnant. Then we secured each with pieces of twine. They made portable forget-me-nots for guests to snack on later. At other parties, we've gifted dulce de leche and Montse's mango jam. Pick up the ramekins for less than a dollar each at kitchen-supply stores.

juicy fruit

We served an array of tropical juices, such as tamarind, guava, mango, papaya, guanabana (soursop), guayaba, mamey, and coconut water. Bodegas, and even many grocery stores, carry convenient individual-size servings. Goya is a popular brand.

decked out

Canasta is a fun rummy-like game. It hails from Uruguay and calls for two decks of cards, including the jokers. Many long summer nights in Miami are spent playing canasta. *Brisca* and *alcade,* which use Spanish cards, are more fast-paced card games. For instructions and rules on how to play these and other games, visit www.pagat.com.

malta

Long before Coca-Cola became omnipresent in Latin America and the Caribbean, there was malta, a rich nonalcoholic malt beverage that many Latins still drink. We served Malta India from Puerto Rico in honor of Leticia's roots. Plus, the bottles' labels are pretty, so they looked nice on the table. You can find them in bodegas, some grocery stores, and online.

cuban crackers

Thin and crispy, Cuban crackers—*galletas* or *galleticas*—taste like crunchy Cuban bread. My dad used to make them using leftover Cuban bread dough. Also called water or marine crackers, because they have a long shelf life, they come in all sizes, tiny ones perfect for soup toppings, medium ones for dips, and large ones for extra-crunchy cracker sandwiches. Some popular brands include Rika and Gilda.

BEATS

When our grandmothers used to get together with their girlfriends to play canasta, old-school love songs and Caribbean waltzes hummed in the background. For this get-together, we tapped boleros from that era, sung masterfully by Gloria Estefan and Juan Carlos Salazar. Then we increased the volume with the emotionally charged sounds of La Lupe and Colombia's Shakira, who masterfully mixes modern Latin pop with Middle Eastern rhythms.

Best of La Lupe
Raíces y Motivos   Hernán Gamboa y Juan Carlos Salazar
Luna   Claudia Acuña
Mi Tierra   Gloria Estefan
Donde Estan Los Ladrones   Shakira

la pampa

AN AFTER-POLO DINNER FOR 8

BECAUSE PART OF MY JOB IS TO REPORT FASHION AND TRENDS, I'VE BEEN LUCKY ENOUGH TO TWICE

visit Buenos Aires. A strong design community, it's a hotbed of stylish people. Pablo Ramirez is one of the country's most successful cutting-edge fashion designers, dressing celebrities and fashionistas, and Frederico de Alzaga makes gorgeous modern silver jewelry. When not working, I explored some of the top spots in the city that they call the Paris of Latin America, falling in love with its French architecture, visiting Casa Rosada (where Eva Perón famously addressed the masses), snapping pictures of tango dancers in the colorful La Boca district, shopping at the immense San Telmo flea market, catering to my inner carnivore with steak and sausages, and enjoying dulce de leche, a delectable sweet milk jam.

For this adventure in the middle of an Argentine winter, we drove an hour south of Buenos Aires to a ranch called Estancia el Rocío, which is home to the charming country inn owned by Patrice Gravière and his wife, Macarena. Set in La Pampa, Argentina's vast grassy plains, the inn has exposed ceiling timbers and whitewashed walls, as well as locally crafted wood furniture and an antique doorframe rescued from a monastery. La Pampa is where Argentine gauchos, or cowboys, live. Like American cowboys, they tend to the ranches, cattle, and horses. The Gravières graciously shared their local customs and life with us: we drank a traditional tea, maté, with their neighbor, Don Melliso, an eighty-year-old gaucho; at an *asado* (an Argentine barbecue) we ate lamb that had been roasted on an iron rack over a bed of red-hot coals; and we saw about twenty polo ponies being broken in and trained for the next season. Patrice even put on a mini-polo game for us to watch, and afterward we celebrated with a South American–themed dinner prepared by Carolina and the Estancia's Uruguayan chef, Ramón Perdomo Sierra. I contributed hearty winter drinks, and we finished with a multitiered dulce de leche cake, which we snacked on all night by the fire.

PONCHE crema

SERVES 6

THIS RECIPE CALLS FOR INSTANT FLAN MIX, which gives this drink a sweet, creamy custard flavor.

One 5.5-ounce package Goya flan mix
    (or a little less than two 3-ounce packages
    of Jell-O mix)
3 cups whole or low-fat milk
One 14-ounce can sweetened condensed milk
2 cups dark rum
Freshly grated nutmeg

Boil the flan mix with 2 cups milk (discard the caramel mix that comes in the box). Chill until it congeals, about an hour. In a blender combine the chilled flan, the sweetened condensed milk, the remaining 1 cup of milk, and the dark rum. Blend and serve in goblets and garnish with freshly grated nutmeg.

Hot Wine

VINO caliente

SERVES 6

THIS IS A HOT, MULLED FULL-BODIED WINE that we made with an Argentine Malbec. Malbec is the red grape from the Mendoza region of western Argentina. The spicy, fruity flavor complements the aromatics.

4 cinnamon sticks
6 whole cloves
⅓ cup sugar
1 bottle Malbec wine
4 slivers of orange rind

Bring the cinnamon, cloves, sugar, and 2½ cups of water to a boil in a large saucepan. Simmer for 5 minutes. Remove from heat and add the wine and orange rinds, and bring to a boil. Simmer on low heat for 5 minutes. Strain and ladle into mugs.

coquito

THIS RICH COCONUT CONFECTION is enjoyed during the Christmas holidays and is also known as Puerto Rican eggnog. Most recipes call for light rum, but my Puerto Rican friend Aida Flamm uses dark rum and brandy for a bit of a kick.

Two 12-ounce cans evaporated milk
Two 14-ounce cans sweetened condensed milk
One 15-ounce can coconut cream, such as
    Coco Lopez
1 liter dark rum
¼ cup brandy
Ground cinnamon
10 cinnamon sticks

Mix all the ingredients, except the cinnamon and cinnamon sticks, in a blender and chill. Serve in goblets or glasses with a sprinkle of cinnamon on top and a cinnamon stick.

ANDEAN milk

SERVES 6

ONE COLD NEW YORK WINTER Carolina shared this recipe with me. Her family would drink it when they'd go to the Venezuelan Andes on vacation. It's commonly served at many mountain inns. It is lightly flavored with cinnamon and vanilla, two distinct Latin flavors, and amaretto, probably the influence of the many Italians who immigrated to Venezuela.

6 cups milk
4 teaspoons ground cinnamon
1 teaspoon vanilla extract
4 ounces amaretto, such as Amaretto
    di Saronno
6 cinnamon sticks

Heat the milk to near boil in a saucepan. Remove from the heat. Whisk in the cinnamon, vanilla, and amaretto. Divide among mugs and garnish with cinnamon sticks.

My maternal grandparents came from Catalonia, in the northeast region of Spain, where this is eaten as a snack, appetizer, or light tapas dish when topped with Serrano ham, chorizo, morcilla (Spanish or Argentine blood sausage), or anchovies. In homage to the many Spaniards who settled in Argentina in the mid-1900s, we served this bread as an appetizer. Tomato bread may be served warm or at room temperature, and can be made up to an hour ahead.

This will serve 8 to 10.

2 baguettes
Extra virgin olive oil
1 garlic clove, peeled
4 medium ripe tomatoes
Salt to taste

Preheat the oven to 300°F.

Slice the baguettes lengthwise. Then cut them into smaller, crosswise 4-inch pieces. Arrange the slices of bread on a foil-lined baking sheet and drizzle the bread generously with olive oil. Bake in the oven for 10 to 12 minutes, or until the tops are a light golden color.

When cool enough to handle, rub the garlic clove across the baked bread. Slice the tomatoes crosswise and rub their fleshy pulp and seeds onto the tops of the bread slices. Add the salt to taste. If desired, drizzle more olive oil just before serving.

CATALAN TOMATO bread

Pa amb Tomàquet

HEARTS OF PALM ARE THE SOFT INSIDES OF THE SABEL PALMETTO TREE, which grows in parts of Central and South America. My mother served these delicacies when we had guests to our home. I adore their velvety texture and earthy taste.

Today most hearts of palm are harvested in Brazil, Costa Rica, Venezuela, and South Florida. While freshly harvested hearts are hard to come by, there are a number of good canned varieties, such as Roland. The dressing may be made up to a day ahead, chilled, and tossed right before serving.

The salad will serve 8.

DRESSING

1 cup plain yogurt
2 tablespoons honey
3 tablespoons freshly squeezed lime juice
1 teaspoon finely chopped dill
Salt and freshly ground black pepper to taste

SALAD

12 to 14 hearts of palm (one 7.75-ounce can), drained and thickly sliced
2 cucumbers, peeled and thinly sliced
2 plum tomatoes, cut into wedges

Combine all the dressing ingredients in a bowl, whisk with a fork, cover, and chill. Arrange the salad ingredients in a larger bowl when ready to serve. Toss with the dressing, and add more salt and pepper if desired.

HEARTS OF PALM SALAD WITH DILL-YOGURT dressing

THIS CORN PIE IS THE PERFECT DISH to warm up your guests on a cold winter day. *Choclo* means "corn" in Chile, Argentina, Peru, and Bolivia. In other countries, like Venezuela, corn is called *maíz*. Though this pie is thought of as the national dish of Chile, Peru and Bolivia have their own versions, often substituting chicken for beef or using a combination of both. When I have left-over Thanksgiving turkey, I shred it and use it as a filling for a *pastel de choclo*.

It can be baked in any gratin dish that is at least 8 × 8 inches. You can also make it in small, single-serving gratin dishes, which will take about 15 minutes less to cook.

This will serve 8.

FILLING

2 tablespoons vegetable or corn oil
2 medium yellow onions, finely chopped
3 garlic cloves, minced
1 pound ground lean beef
2 teaspoons cumin powder
Salt to taste
2 teaspoons (preferably sweet) Spanish
    smoked paprika (see page 9)

PASTEL de choclo

Chilean Corn Pie

CORN TOPPING

Three 16-ounce bags frozen yellow corn kernels
  (about 6½ cups), thawed and rinsed
¼ cup milk
6 large basil leaves
About ½ teaspoon ground nutmeg,
  more or less to taste
1 tablespoon salt
1 tablespoon sugar
3 tablespoons butter
1 egg, lightly beaten
Salt and freshly ground black pepper to taste
2 hard-boiled eggs, crumbled
¼ cup raisins
½ cup chopped green olives (preferably stuffed
  with red pimiento), drained
1½ tablespoons confectioners' sugar

In a large skillet, heat the oil. Add the onions and sauté over medium heat until tender, about 7 minutes. Add the garlic, beef, cumin, and salt. Cook until the beef browns, stirring occasionally and breaking it up with a wooden spoon as necessary.

Remove the beef from the heat, stir in half the paprika, and then drain the meat through a medium-mesh sieve colander lined with cheesecloth or paper towels, to remove the excess liquid.

Preheat the oven to 375°F.

To prepare the corn topping, combine the corn, milk, basil, nutmeg, salt, and sugar in a food processor. Pulse until it's slightly lumpy, about the consistency of oatmeal. You may need to do this in two batches.

In a medium saucepan, melt the butter over low heat. Add the corn puree and the beaten egg, stirring until the mixture thickens and bubbles, 5 to 7 minutes. Remove from the heat. Adjust the salt and pepper to taste.

Layer a gratin dish with the prepared beef, followed by a layer of the crumbled hard-boiled eggs, raisins, and olives. Top with the corn mixture, smoothing the surface with a spatula. Using a small sifter, evenly sprinkle the top of the pie with the confectioners' sugar and the remaining teaspoon of paprika.

Bake at 375°F for 30 to 45 minutes, or until the top turns golden brown.

Alfajor de Mil Capas

THOUSAND-LAYER alfajor

AS A TELECOM ENGINEER, MY FATHER TRAVELS ALL OVER LATIN AMERICA. When we were little, my brother and I would ransack his suitcase looking for gifts from his trips. Once we got Bolivian parkas made from alpaca. From Mexico he brought back papier-mâché masks, and from Argentina a box of alfajores that Mom rationed out. Alfajores are two small butter cookies bound by dulce de leche filling. They're sold in pastry shops throughout Argentina, Uruguay, and Paraguay.

The dessert we served at this party is a decadent, daring, and dramatic interpretation of the diminutive alfajor. Full disclosure: This skyscraper of a cake takes time and dexterity. Make it one to two days before a party. Alternatively, you can make the disks ahead and store them in an airtight container for up to two weeks.

As for the dulce de leche filling, it can be made up to a week in advance, refrigerated, and then brought to room temperature. If you don't want to make dulce de leche from scratch, it's sold canned in grocery stores and at online retailers.

This recipe comes from Ramón Perdomo Sierra, the chef of El Rocío. I'm grateful to him for letting me apprentice in his kitchen and for sharing his *Alfajor de Mil Capas* recipe.

This recipe will make up to 26 cake layers and will serve 10 people. You can also make two shorter 12-layer cakes that will serve 20.

ALFAJOR LAYERS

7¼ cups all-purpose flour
7 large egg yolks (reserve the whites for the icing)
2 large whole eggs
3 tablespoons sugar
3 tablespoons vodka or gin
Pinch of salt
2¼ sticks (9 ounces) unsalted butter, melted
Flour for dusting

FILLING

Three 13.4-ounce cans dulce de leche (or dulce de leche, page 46)

MERINGUE ICING

3 cups sugar
7 egg whites
⅛ teaspoon cream of tartar

Combine the flour, yolks, whole eggs, sugar, vodka, and salt in the bowl of a mixer with a dough hook attachment. (You may also knead by hand, but it will take three times as long.) Knead on speed 1 for 8 minutes, and slowly add ¼ cup water. The dough will start to look crumbly. While the mixer is on, slowly drizzle in the melted butter. Add ½ cup water and continue kneading until the dough comes together, about 5 minutes.

Transfer the dough to a well-floured surface and, with your hands, knead for a couple more minutes so that it is one smooth ball. Place the dough in a large bowl, cover with a kitchen towel, and let it rest in a non-drafty place (such as a microwave) for 30 minutes.

Punch the dough. On a well-floured surface, knead the dough until it becomes elastic. Divide in half, and divide one of the halves into small balls (about 2½ inches in diameter). With a rolling pin, roll out each ball until it is a very thin circle, about 9 inches round.

Place the bottom of an 8-inch springform pan or round cake pan on each circular disk and trace a circle with the tip of a paring knife. (Save the dough trimmings to make more disks.) Set the disks on a plate, sprinkle lightly with flour, and cover the plate with a kitchen towel.

Once you've cut out about 16 disks, preheat the oven to 400°F.

Once you've made all 26 disks, take them out one at a time and, using a rolling pin, stretch them so that they are approximately 9 inches in diameter. Prick the disks all over with a fork and place on one or two cookie sheets. Make sure to prick liberally or else you will end up with large air bubbles. Bake the disks in the center of the oven for 2 to 3 minutes, or until they turn a light tan color. Remove and cool on a wire rack, and cool the cookie sheets between baking. If the oven door remains open for too long, allow the temperature to reset to 400°F. Continue baking the remaining disks.

Once baked, stack them—in short piles, so they don't break—on a plate or cooling rack. When the cookie disks are at room temperature, place the largest one you can find on the bottom of a cake stand and spread a thin layer of dulce de leche on it. Add another cookie disk, more dulce de leche, and so on, until you reach the top. Now make the icing.

In a small saucepan, heat the sugar and 1 cup water on low, stirring to dissolve. Bring to a boil and continue to heat until the sugar syrup reaches the "soft-ball stage," or 240°F on a candy thermometer. This should take 6 to 7 minutes.

While the sugar is boiling, beat the egg whites and cream of tartar on high until foamy. Lower the mixer speed and carefully pour the sugar syrup along the side of the mixer. Increase the mixer speed to medium-high and beat the meringue until glossy, stiff peaks form.

Wait a couple of minutes until the mixing bowl has slightly cooled and then fill a pastry bag with the meringue icing. Using a medium, smooth tip, pipe out the icing in rivulets on top of the *Alfajor de Mil Capas*. This cake should be served at room temperature.

gauchos

Gauchos are the cowboys of Latin America, tending to the land and herding horses and livestock. Two gauchos that we met—Jota and Melliso—still adhere to the old way of life: They travel by horse, wear customary leather broad-brimmed hats or berets, ponchos (which are used as blankets at night), and baggy *bombacha* pants, often tucked into boots crafted from the hide of the back legs of colts. As if these men weren't stylish enough, they frequently wear a scarf fashioned like an ascot. At our *asado,* Jota carved the roasted lamb using an ornate *facón,* or large knife, that gauchos tuck into their wide leather belts.

polo

Today Argentina is the polo player's mecca. Polo made its way to Latin America via British settlers, and Buenos Aires is home to the world's most prestigious polo tournament, the Argentine Open, which draws tens of thousands of spectators. Throughout the season, which runs from October to March, El Rocío's huge polo fields are filled with international players looking to improve their game and to watch the Open. Our match, with Patrice's friends and family, was just for fun.

maté

Made from the leaves of a bush native to Paraguay and environs, maté is served in a hollowed-out gourd. Drinkers share the strong, bitter hot tea, sipping it from a single *bombilla*, a kind of straw with a small infusion chamber at its base. It is a stimulant and often drunk in lieu of coffee. To drink maté is to accept a gesture of friendship, warmth, and welcome. In Argentina the tea is oftened sweetened with sugar or honey, while in Uruguay it is frequently served unsweetened.

vino latino

Latin America has been producing wine since the 1500s, when Spanish missionaries began planting vineyards throughout the continent. Argentina's verdant Mendoza region in the west is known for its fruity Malbecs, like those produced by the Dolium winery. Chile's Cousiño Macul winery, from the oldest wine family in that country, exports excellent Chardonnays, among other varietals. Further north, the dry Baja region of Mexico produces lush Merlots from Bodegas de Santo Tomás estate and full-bodied Zinfandels from neighboring Château Camou.

It is also noteworthy that many Latinos have made their mark on vineyards in the United States, especially in California, where a number of wineries are owned and operated by former Mexican migrant workers. The Robledo Family Winery is one, producing award-winning wines from Sonoma and Napa Valley.

tagged

Bottling mulled wine, *ponche crema*, or coquito for gift-giving is easy. We washed out old wine bottles and funneled in our homemade beverages. We also ordered a personalized stamp online and impressed our good tidings on store-bought tags. Or, handwrite warm wishes on small note cards, punch a hole at a corner of each one, and tie them to the bottles' necks with a small string or ribbon.

gorgeous gourds

Since our after-polo dinner party took place in the middle of winter, we dressed the table with a collection of colorful gourds and filled vases with Brazilian lemons—they look like tangerines, but taste like limes—picked from trees in the backyard. Decorating tables with fruits and vegetables works no matter what the season. Fill bowls and plates with pineapples, lemons, oranges, kumquats, or artichokes at your next event.

mix and match

San Telmo's flea market is a collector's dream. We bought inexpensive old wooden candlesticks and added them to Macarena's collection of new and inherited ones for the rustic table setting. Flea markets and thrift stores are great places for inexpensive and cool finds from all over the world.

olives

The quintessential Spanish and Latin American tapa. At this party, we served green Spanish manzanilla olives, available in most grocery stores. They come pitted as well as stuffed with pimiento, anchovies, almonds, jalapeños, or garlic.

BEATS

In addition to classic and new tango, we played the youthful sounds of Argentine reggae band Los Pericos. We also threw in a shimmy-all-night compilation that is *Brown Sugar,* a favorite for all generations.

The Best of Carlos Gardel
Tango: Zero Hour   Astor Piazzolla
Pampas Reggae   Los Pericos
Tango Varón   Sandra Luna
Brown Sugar Break Beats, Basslines and
   Boogaloo

a pool party

in puerto rico

A CARIBBEAN TAPAS MENU FOR 4 OR MORE

FROM A LOUNGE AT JFK, WE DIALED OUR GLAMOROUS GAL PAL, DEBORAH CARTHY-DEU, ALERTING HER THAT WE WERE EN ROUTE TO HER ISLAND.

Who better to show us the goings-on about town than the affable former Miss Universe? After she was crowned in 1985, Deborah traveled the world; but when it came time to settle down, she was on the first plane to Puerto Rico.

American citizens may not need a passport to visit Puerto Rico, but once you arrive you'll know you're not in Kansas anymore. The minutes tick slower, the sun beats stronger, and the people brim with *espíritu*. Streets are never still: The echo of a salsa beat flows from a balcony, briefly overshadowed by a car stereo blasting American pop tunes. In the busy cafés, you hear clips of English phrases, then a succession of rapid-fire Spanish dialogue. A group of schoolboys out for the night whistle at a pretty passerby.

Isabel and I have many dear friends in Puerto Rico, and since the flights from New York in summer are inexpensive, we often pack our bags for a weekend of sightseeing, eating, and partying. Once we landed in San Juan, Deborah and her friend Luz drove us to San Felipe del Morro, a six-level fortress skirting Old San Juan. The fortress protected the city against invaders for centuries, including a vicious attack by Sir Francis Drake. Today it flaunts some of the most panoramic vistas of the island's blue waters.

Upon entering Old San Juan, we walked down its cobblestone streets crowded with old Spanish homes. We stopped at a plaza filled with domino players and then enjoyed some *piraguas*, flavored ices, from a local street vendor. When I was growing up, they used to be served at pool parties. And that got me thinking . . . *when was* the last time I'd been to a pool party?

The next morning Isabel and I mapped out the details of our next shindig. Time: One o'clock. Place: The Water Club Hotel's rooftop pool. Dress: Swimsuit, towel, cover-up, and plenty of sunscreen.

Isabel decided to forgo paper plates in lieu of white sushi plates. Meanwhile, I came up with a light, multicultural tapas menu. Our friend Emil Rivera prepared a traditional Puerto Rican Mofongo with Crabmeat Ceviche. Isabel shook up dozens of heavenly coconut martinis. Sultry salsa beats and Latin rock tunes set the mood.

As the party got under way, we splashed around the pool with campy beach balls and baked under the Caribbean's very own heat lamp.

COCONUT martini

SERVES 2

THE WATER CLUB'S SPECIALTY DRINK features a double dose of coconut from the cream and the coconut-flavored rum.

4 ounces coconut cream, chilled,
    such as Coco Lopez
6 ounces vodka
1 ounce coconut rum, such as Bacardi Coco
Ground cinnamon
2 cinnamon sticks

Combine all the ingredients, except the ground cinnamon and cinnamon sticks, in a shaker filled with ice. Shake and strain into martini glasses. Garnish with a pinch of cinnamon and a cinnamon stick.

GLORIMAR

SERVES 2

THIS PLEASING BEVERAGE IS INSPIRED BY our Puerto Rican friend Glorimar Alvarez. Her husband, a manager at the Water Club, makes a version with passion fruit juice, so feel free to swap. Angostura bitters are good to add to a drink if it's too sweet, or if you want a touch of spice. A doctor looking for a digestive aid invented the alcoholic herbal elixir in Venezuela, but now it's mostly used as a flavoring for food and drinks. It's extra strong (and bitter), so a dash will do.

4 ounces mango juice
3 ounces light rum
2 ounces amaretto, such as
    Amaretto di Saronno
Dash of bitters
Grapes (optional)

Combine all the ingredients, except the grapes, in a shaker filled with ice. Shake and strain into chilled martini glasses. Garnish with grapes, if desired.

CABANA boy

A COCONUT TWIST ON A CUBA LIBRE.

2 ounces coconut rum, such as Bacardi Coco
Coca-Cola
Lime wedge

Pour the rum and Coke into a highball glass filled with ice (about 2 parts Coke to 1 part rum). Squeeze in the lime wedge, give a stir, and drop it in.

WHISKEY a CO-CO

SERVES I

THIS IS A SMOOTH CONCOCTION FOR THOSE who don't want a sweet drink. Coconut water is the liquid from a young green coconut. Vita Coco, a Brazilian brand, is sold at grocery stores and online.

2 ounces coconut water
2 ounces Scotch, such as Dewar's Scotch Whiskey

Pour the coconut water and Scotch in an old-fashioned glass filled with ice. Stir and enjoy.

SLIM ASPARAGUS SPEARS PAIR NICELY with bold, caviar-flavored aïoli. The price of caviar varies—from exorbitantly expensive Russian beluga (up to one hundred dollars an ounce) to the more accessible American varieties (starting at eight dollars an ounce) that come from white sturgeon, hackleback, or paddlefish. I always use American caviar for this recipe. We fancied adding caviar to aïoli after discovering Marky's, an incredible Russian store north of downtown Miami.

Both the asparagus and the aïoli may be made up to a day ahead and stored in the refrigerator until serving.

This will serve 4.

20 medium asparagus spears
2 ounces black caviar
Aïoli
Plum tomatoes, for garnish (optional)

Peel the lower half of the asparagus spears with a vegetable peeler. Cook the asparagus spears in a wide pot of boiling salted water until just tender, 6 to 8 minutes. Drain and soak the asparagus in ice water (to lock in the bright green color) for just a few seconds. Chill.

Before serving, gently fold 1½ to 2 teaspoons of the black caviar into the aïoli. Arrange five spears per person with a spoonful of aïoli. Garnish with extra caviar and sliced plum tomatoes, if desired.

ASPARAGUS SPEARS WITH AÏOLI caviar dip

Aïoli

AÏOLI, A SPANISH GARLICKY SAUCE with the consistency of mayonnaise, is served with boiled potatoes, French fries, beef, chicken, and fish, or slathered on sandwiches. This recipe may be made up to a day ahead and refrigerated.

This makes about 1 cup of aïoli.

2 small garlic cloves, peeled
1 teaspoon salt
1 large egg yolk
½ teaspoon Dijon mustard
1 tablespoon white wine vinegar
1 cup extra virgin olive oil, or more to taste

In a mortar and pestle, mash the garlic and salt into a paste. Transfer to a large bowl with a round bottom. Whisk the paste with the egg yolk, mustard, and vinegar until incorporated, and then vigorously continue to whisk as you pour in a narrow, steady stream of olive oil. The oil must be added bit by bit or else the aïoli will curdle.

Note: Aïoli may also be made in a blender by mixing the garlic paste, egg yolk, mustard, and vinegar, and then slowly pouring in the olive oil.

To make more than a cup of aïoli, just whisk in more oil and it will expand. Store the aïoli in the refrigerator, covered. Use within a couple of days.

WHEN ISABEL'S PARENTS OWNED A RESTAURANT, this nontraditional sandwich was as big a hit as the ubiquitous Cuban sandwich. It was Isabel's favorite when she was little. Here we offer it as a mini-tapas version.

One prepared loaf will serve 4 to 6.

Whole-grain mustard
1 loaf Cuban or French bread, diagonally sliced, about ½ inch thick
1 Spanish or Mexican chorizo sausage (9.5 ounces), diagonally sliced, casings removed
1 large yellow onion, thinly sliced
Salt to taste
Olive oil

red spaniard sandwich

Spread the mustard on half the bread slices, which will form the bottoms of the sandwich.

Heat a cast-iron skillet or other heavy skillet and cook the chorizo slices for 4 to 5 minutes over medium heat. Remove them with a slotted spoon and set aside in a bowl. In the chorizo oil, sauté the onion slices until they are soft. Sprinkle with salt and place them in the same bowl with the chorizo.

Top all the mustardy sandwich bottoms with a layer of chorizo and onion. Cover with the bread tops. Any remaining chorizo and onion can be used for garnish.

In a clean skillet over low to medium heat, heat enough olive oil to just coat the surface. Place as many prepared mini-sandwiches as the skillet will hold (4 to 5) and flatten them with either a sandwich press or another skillet. Cook until each side is lightly golden, about 1½ minutes per side. Repeat with the remaining sandwiches. Serve warm.

Ceviches, citrus-marinated seafood, may occupy the culinary annals of many Latin American countries, but in Peru making ceviche is an art form. Its preparation varies from one coastal town to another. Some recipes call for the fish to be marinated for hours in fresh lime juice, breaking down the proteins and essentially cooking the fish; other recipes call for topping the fish with a citrus dressing just before serving. The latter results in a more raw, sashimi-like texture. Sounds Asian? Perhaps it's due to the huge Chinese and Japanese migrations to Peru that occurred in the late nineteenth century.

In flavoring their ceviches, Peruvians use a wide variety of *ajís,* or peppers. Popular *ajís* include the red and spicy rocoto pepper, or the fruity and fiery yellow mirasol pepper (also sold as Peruvian *ají amarillo*). In this version, I use a mirasol pepper, which is sold canned, dried, or in a paste. If using the paste, two teaspoons should provide enough heat.

While this is a tasting plate for 4, in Peru it could serve as a meal if accompanied by boiled sweet potatoes and corn.

PERUVIAN TUNA CEVICHE WITH MIRASOL PEPPER and kiwi

1 kiwi fruit, peeled and thinly sliced, for garnish

DRESSING

1 medium Peruvian mirasol pepper (dried or canned), cored and seeded
Juice of 6 limes (about ½ cup)
½ red bell pepper, minced
3 tablespoons minced shallot
1 teaspoon grated gingerroot
1 tablespoon chopped, flat-leaf parsley
Salt and freshly ground black pepper to taste
1 pound sushi-grade tuna, cubed into roughly 1-inch pieces
Handful of chives, thinly sliced, for garnish
A few drops lemon-infused oil (optional), for garnish

Line the kiwi slices decoratively on tasting plates. Cover with plastic wrap and refrigerate until ready to serve the ceviche.

If using a dried mirasol pepper, rehydrate the pepper (see page 105).

Finely chop and combine the mirasol pepper in a bowl with the lime juice, bell pepper, shallot, gingerroot, parsley, and salt and pepper. Refrigerate.

Minutes before serving, stir the dressing, toss with the tuna pieces, and serve immediately on the chilled kiwi plates. Garnish with the sliced chives and lemon oil, if desired.

MOFONGO WITH crabmeat ceviche

BORN IN SAN JUAN, EMIL RIVERA IS THE TWENTY-FOUR-YEAR-OLD SOUS CHEF at the Water Club Hotel, where Isabel and I hosted our pool party. Their menu is a sleek fusion of Asian techniques with Caribbean ingredients, but at home Emil cooks the traditional island fare he grew up with, including mofongo, a dish of warm plantains mashed with garlic and bacon or *chicharrón* (pork crackling). In this version, Emil topped his mofongo with chilled crabmeat ceviche. Mofongo may be made up to a day ahead and reheated in a pot with some chicken stock to moisten it. *Chicharrones* can be found in Latin markets.

This will serve 4.

CRABMEAT CEVICHE

4 ounces lump or flaked crabmeat, picked over
1 teaspoon finely chopped cilantro
1 scallion, thinly sliced on the diagonal
1 jalapeño, cored, seeded, and sliced into
    long slivers
Pinch of cumin

1 teaspoon olive oil
1 teaspoon vinegar
Juice of 1 lime
Salt and freshly ground black pepper

With your hands, roughly shred the crabmeat into smaller pieces. Combine all of the ingredients in a bowl, toss, cover with plastic wrap, and chill for 4 hours or overnight. Remove from the refrigerator a half hour before serving.

MOFONGO

2 unripe, unpeeled green plantains, cut into
   1-inch rounds
Vegetable oil
2 bacon strips, or ¼ cup *chicharrones*,
   roughly chopped
2 garlic cloves
1½ to 2 cups low-sodium chicken stock,
   warmed
Salt
1 tablespoon finely chopped cilantro,
   for garnish
A few snipped chives (optional), for garnish

Soak the plantain rounds in salted water to cover for 15 minutes. Drain and pat dry. Using a knife, cut off and remove their hard green peels. Heat a heavy skillet with a depth of 1 inch of oil. When the oil is hot, fry the plantains on medium heat for about 5 minutes, or until they are golden but not brown. Remove them with a slotted spoon to a paper towel–lined plate.

Mash the plantains in a bowl with a fork, until they are a chunky consistency.

In a non-oiled pan, fry the bacon strips until crispy. When cool enough to handle, crumble them over the plantains. Cook the garlic in the bacon grease until it begins to turn golden. Remove and mash with a fork. In the bowl of plantains, mix together the bacon and garlic. Pour about a cup and a half of the warm chicken stock to moisten the plantain mash. The plantains will soak up the stock. Add salt to taste.

Plate the mofongo in small bowls using an ice-cream scooper. Top with the crab ceviche, cilantro, and chives, if desired. Add a couple of tablespoons of the warm chicken stock into the bottom of the bowl to moisten the mofongo just before serving.

PAPAYA CREAM WITH crème de cassis

RASCAL, A RESTAURANT IN SÃO PAULO, BRAZIL, serves the best papaya cream topped with deep purple swirls of crème de cassis. When I saw the large, ripe papayas for sale in a fruit market in Old San Juan, I had to make this dessert for our party. It was such a hit that by the end of the day, as more friends arrived, I had made three batches.

Two types of papayas are available in North America: the Hawaiian pear-shaped papaya, with its bright yellow-orange flesh, and the larger Caribbean papaya, with its salmon-colored flesh. The shiny black seeds on the inside are edible and have a peppery taste. Use them to garnish any number of sweet or savory dishes.

This will serve 4.

3 cups peeled, seeded, and chopped papaya
    (about 18 ounces or a little less than
    a small papaya)
6 scoops vanilla ice cream (about 12 ounces)
Crème de cassis (black currant liqueur)

Puree the papaya and ice cream in a blender or food processor until smooth.

Divide the portions of the papaya mixture into dessert bowls and serve immediately. Drizzle about a tablespoon of crème de cassis over each. Alternatively, place a shot glass of cassis on the side for each guest to serve themselves.

Any leftover papaya may be cut into small cubes for snacking.

cerveza, please!

Fill a large tub with ice and a selection of beers from Latin America and the Caribbean, such as:

Argentina	Quilmes
Brazil	Brahma, Xingu, Antartica, Sambadoro
Colombia	Águila
Costa Rica	Imperial
Dominican Republic	Presidente
El Salvador	Cantina
Guatemala	Gallo, Famosa
Mexico	Sol, Pacifico, Tecate
Nicaragua	Victoria, Toña
Panama	Soberana, Panamá
Peru	Cerveza Cristal, Pilsen Callao, Cusqueña
Puerto Rico	Tesoro
Venezuela	Polar

nice ice

Not even water and ice are safe from our meddling! We froze fresh mint leaves and berries in ice cubes for the water that we served. The touch gave the water a subtle hint of flavor, and it made for a simple, effortless, yet elegant presentation.

stone age

On windy days, use smooth river stones to prevent napkins from flying away. We bought ours by the bag for a few dollars at a local nursery and tied them with a few red leather strips from a craft store. We made necklaces with the smaller rocks by tightly tying extra leather around them.

green piece

For outdoor spring and summer gatherings, use fresh leaves as drink coasters. We picked these from the bushes right outside the hotel. Any leaf that is smooth, flat, and slightly thick will do the trick.

what a heel

Take a chance and wear heels the next time you sport your bathing suit and sarong at the pool. Sandals, like the ones by Puerto Rican designer Edmundo Castillo, lengthen legs and are supersexy. If you'll be walking a lot, just throw some flip-flops in your purse.

one hot dish

There's no need to use paper plates anymore, because sushi plates are inexpensive and sleek, easy to wash, and you can reuse them party after party. They are available online or at houseware and restaurant-supply stores.

piraguas

Whether you are in Puerto Rico, Cuba, Venezuela, or any other Caribbean country, you'll likely run into street vendors selling these tropical fruit–flavored ices. They have different names, depending where you are. In Puerto Rico, they're *piraguas;* in Venezuela, *raspaos;* and in Cuba, *granizados.*

hot head

Stay cool in the shade with a sexy straw hat, like this one, which we picked up at a beach store in Puerto Rico. They make great party favors. Another option are famous Panama hats, which, despite the name, do not come from Panama—they are from Ecuador. These handmade straw hats come in a variety of styles, from the classic fedora to the wider-brimmed planter style. The price depends on its weave. The most tightly woven hats are the best and most expensive. Buy Panama hats at www.panamahatsdirect.com.

dominoes

This tile game is believed to have originated in fourteenth-century China and made its way to eighteenth-century Venetian courts. We may not know whom to credit for inventing dominoes, but we do know that today it is beloved in Latin America. In many towns and cities, men (and the occasional woman) play dominoes in town plazas in the early morning or late afternoon, when the sun is not too strong.

It is also a popular game played at gatherings. Usually a host will bring out a couple of sets of dominoes and a tray with after-dinner drinks. Guests pair up and play for hours.

For rules on how to play dominoes, go to www.mastersgames.com.

BEATS

Puerto Ricans respect their musical roots, as well as rocking to new homegrown acts. From Puerto Rican legend Gilberto Santa Rosa, known as El Caballero de la Salsa, to poppy Shalim and reggaetón, at this pool party we swam between old and new school.

Autentico   Gilberto Santa Rosa
Mad Love   Robi Draco Rosa
Vivanativa   Vivanativa
Cuarto Sin Puerta   Shalim
El Abayarde   Tego Calderón

celebrating

mexico:
art, food,
and culture

AN ARTSY LUNCH FOR 8

MEXICO IS A VAST NATION, FILLED WITH MUCH BEAUTY AND DIVERSITY IN ITS HISTORY, PEOPLE, CULTURE,

and food. I got a small taste of the country when my sister Ofelia lived in Mexico City. I visited her, and together we explored, zipping around in her little VW Bug. We climbed steep pyramids, ate tacos at roadside stands, navigated crowded markets, and gazed at behemoth Aztec sculptures and Diego Rivera storybook murals. I've been back a few times since she left, to hit the spots we missed. After college, I backpacked around the Yucatán, where the soft white-sand beaches were prettier than any I've seen. A few years later, I made it to the Pacific Coast around Acapulco and Puerto Vallarta, where I comically tried to surf the big waves and thoroughly enjoyed an introduction to a spicy Asian-inspired margarita unlike any I'd had before. And there are still so many places I haven't been to yet. Who knows if I'll ever get to see it all, but Carolina and I were thrilled to be invited to see the picturesque town of Cuernavaca through the eyes of our friends Sully Bonnelly and Robert Littman one summer weekend.

Dominican-born fashion designer Sully and Mexico-based art expert and collector Robert live in the hillside home once occupied by their friends and fellow art patrons Natasha and Jacques Gelman. A few years ago, Robert was charged with managing the Gelmans' library of works, and under his aegis, it has grown to include more than 320 important pieces, including paintings by Frida Kahlo and Diego Rivera. Lucky for us, our trip meant a tour of the Cuernavaca museum where Robert's collection is currently housed. In return for an art lesson and their hospitality, we arranged for an artfully prepared Mexican lunch on the terrace overlooking their beautiful bougainvillea-bathed garden. We also invited Gerardo Suter, a photographer whose works are hanging in the museum.

For the feast, Carolina prepared a few of her favorite Mexican dishes, including a delicious cochinita pibil, a traditional pork dish from the Yucatán. I dug out the Szechwan Margarita recipe from Puerto Vallarta. Gerardo's wife, Gerda, made the most amazing Cuernavacan dish ever—chicken wrapped in fresh-picked, bright pumpkin blossoms, with mole sauce. In honor of the cultural feel of the weekend, I added a few iconic and colorful Mexican elements to the table. But you don't need to go all the way to Mexico to celebrate its cultural and culinary offerings. Here's a secret: I bought the table toppers at craft stores in New York and Atlanta.

SULLY AND ROBERT SERVED US THIS ELEGANT DRINK created in honor of their friend Natasha Gelman. Natasha liked the watermelon's ruby hue and iconic association with her adopted country. You'll need watermelon juice to make this, so if you can't find it at the grocery store, you can easily make it. Take 6 cups of seedless watermelon pulp (about a quarter of a medium watermelon) and liquefy it in a blender. Then run the puree through a cheesecloth or clean tea towel. It will yield about 4 cups of juice.

4 cups watermelon juice, chilled
2 cups cava or other sparkling wine

Pour the juice into a pitcher and stir in the cava. Serve in champagne glasses.

THE natasha
SERVES 6

THE MARGARITA IS ONE OF THE MOST UBIQUITOUS DRINKS in the United States. There are traditional lime margaritas and sweeter versions, such as strawberry, pomegranate, and mango margaritas. This version, a fiery take on the traditional, was invented at Archie's Wok, a popular Asian-fusion restaurant in Puerto Vallarta.

The key ingredient is the chile-infused tequila, which has to be made at least three days in advance.

Steep 5 whole serrano peppers and 5 whole jalapeño peppers for at least 3 days in 1 liter of aged tequila (which is generally smoother tasting than white or silver tequila). Do not refrigerate. Leave it in a slightly cool, dark place, like a cabinet. Watch out, though: the longer the tequila steeps, the hotter it gets.

3 tablespoons superfine sugar
1 cup freshly squeezed lime juice
    (about 10 limes)
1⅓ cups spicy tequila
1 cup Cointreau or other orange liqueur
Salt

Combine the sugar and lime juice in a pitcher. Add the tequila and Cointreau and stir. Pour into old-fashioned glasses that are filled with ice and rimmed with salt.

SZECHWAN margarita

SERVES 4

Hibiscus Tea
AGUA de jamaica
SERVES 6

WITH ITS PURPLE HUE, hibiscus tea is a colorful alternative to regular iced tea. You can buy hibiscus tea at online stores, such as www.theteastore.com, or at local gourmet coffeeshops. You can also substitute Celestial Seasoning's Red Zinger tea, which is made with hibiscus, rosehips, and lemon grass.

⅓ cup sugar
12 hibiscus teabags (2 grams each)

Bring 6 cups water to a boil in a saucepan. Remove from the heat, add the sugar, and steep the teabags. Cover the pan. Once it's cool, remove the teabags and refrigerate in a pitcher until chilled. Pour over ice and enjoy.

michelada
SERVES 1

THERE ARE MANY WAYS TO MAKE THIS SPICY BEER DRINK. The basic ingredients are Mexican beer, lime juice, and salt. Some recipes call for Worcestershire, soy, and/or Maggi sauce, but I prefer to keep it simple. I also use light beers that don't bury the other flavors, though some Mexicans use darker beers, like Negra Modelo, for a richer taste.

Salt
Chili powder, such as McCormick's Chili
    Powder
2 limes, quartered
One 12-ounce bottle of beer, such as Corona
Dash of hot pepper sauce, such as
    Tabasco Brand Chipotle flavor

Combine equal parts salt and chili powder on a flat plate. Rim a beer mug in this mixture. Squeeze the juice of the limes into the mug and toss in a few of the wedges. Fill the mug with beer and top with a dash of hot pepper sauce.

MEXICAN hot chocolate

SERVES 4

OUR FRIEND GREG RAMOS MAKES THE BEST MEXICAN HOT CHOCOLATE. While it's not as thick or as spicy as ones I've had in some regions of Mexico, like Oaxaca, his recipe is a good compromise for those of us more accustomed to thin, sweet, American-style hot cocoa. Some traditional versions of this drink call for whole chile pepper, which at first may seem strange, but the peppery punch actually complements the drink's chocolate bite. Greg suggests adding just a few pinches of chili powder for a little kick. Traditional recipes also call for *canela,* which is the Spanish word for "cinnamon." But Mexican *canela* is really Ceylon, a slightly sweeter cinnamon. If you can find *canela,* use it instead of cinnamon.

1 quart milk
1 cinnamon stick
¼ pound Mexican chocolate, such as Ibarra,
    or semi-sweet chocolate, such as Nestlé
½ teaspoon dark brown sugar
½ teaspoon sugar
Chili powder

Bring the milk and cinnamon stick to a slow boil. Reduce the heat and simmer for 3 minutes. Remove the cinnamon stick and slowly add the chocolate to the milk, stirring until dissolved. Stir in the sugars. Slowly add pinches of chili powder to add punch. Pour into mugs and enjoy.

CHIPS and salsa

WHAT MEXICAN PARTY WOULD BE COMPLETE without chips and salsa? I've included a traditional Mexican salsa as well as a South American one. They're great for dipping store-bought corn tortillas.

salsa cruda

THIS RECIPE FOR MEXICAN SALSA, also called *pico de gallo,* goes well with chips and as an accompaniment to steak and baked chicken. Serve it the same day.

This recipe makes about 3½ cups.

3 large ripe tomatoes, finely chopped
1 medium Spanish onion, finely chopped
2 jalapeño peppers, seeded, cored,
   and finely chopped
2 tablespoons finely chopped cilantro
Juice of ½ lime
Pinch of sugar
Salt

A few hours before serving, mix the ingredients to blend the flavors. Serve at room temperature.

salsa verde

THIS SALSA IS POPULAR IN THE COASTAL TOWNS of Colombia and Venezuela, where it is spooned over stewed meats or seafood. This salsa will keep refrigerated for up to two days.

This recipe makes about 2 cups.

2 Italian peppers (long, mild green peppers),
   finely chopped
1 small onion, finely chopped
3 scallions, green and white parts,
   finely chopped
¼ cup apple cider vinegar
Pinch of sugar
Salt and freshly ground black pepper to taste

Mix all the ingredients well and marinate, covered, in the refrigerator for at least 2 hours.

YUCATÁN pork tacos

TACOS DE COCHINITA PIBIL ARE FOUND EVERYWHERE in the Yucatán peninsula, from street stands in Cancún to fine restaurants in Playa del Carmen. This *cochinita*—or pork—dish dates back to when the Mayans controlled the peninsula and hunted wild boar, marinated it, and cooked it on a spit above ground. *Cochinita* is marinated in achiote paste, which is made from ground annatto seeds and other spices. It gives the pork its distinctive red-brick color. Achiote paste is widely available in Latin markets and online.

Today *cochinita pibil* is often cooked in banana leaves, which not only keep the pork moist and impart a sweet flavor, but make for an eye-popping presentation. Banana leaves are popular in Central American and Caribbean dishes, as well as in Thai and Indonesian cuisine. Ethnic markets and some large grocery chains sell the leaves in the frozen-foods section. If you can't find them, simply wrap the pork in aluminum foil.

While *cochinita* is usually served with flour tortillas, we substitute iceberg lettuce leaves, because we like the crisp texture. This pork dish may be made up to a day ahead and then reheated on the stovetop.

This dish serves 8.

MARINADE

1 dried ancho chile, rehydrated
    (see opposite), cored, and seeded
2 ounces achiote paste
1¼ cups freshly squeezed orange juice
¼ cup freshly squeezed grapefruit juice
¼ cup freshly squeezed lime juice
6 garlic cloves, minced
2 jalapeños, cored, seeded, and minced
2 teaspoons cumin powder
½ teaspoon cinnamon
1 teaspoon dried oregano
1 teaspoon dried thyme
1 tablespoon apple cider vinegar
Few drops of hot pepper sauce,
    such as Tabasco
2 bay leaves
1 teaspoon salt
Pinch of sugar

4 pounds pork shoulder, trimmed and
    quartered
Salt and freshly ground black pepper
1 pound frozen banana leaves, thawed
    (optional)
Kitchen string (optional)
Head of iceberg lettuce, halved,
    leaves separated
Sour cream (optional)
Pickled onions (page 108)

Rehydrate and devein the ancho chile. Slice into thin strips. Break up the achiote paste with a mortar and pestle or meat mallet and then dissolve it in the citrus juices. In a large bowl, combine the remaining marinade ingredients, whisking with a fork until thoroughly mixed.

Reserve and refrigerate 1 cup of the marinade and pour the rest over the pork. Marinate overnight or at least for 4 hours.

When ready to cook the pork, preheat the oven to 275°F.

Line 2 to 3 banana leaves on the bottom of a Dutch oven (or large baking pan with a lid). Lightly salt the pork and place it in the Dutch oven along with any marinade juice. Wrap the pork with the overhanging leaves as if you were wrapping a present, and tie with kitchen string, if desired. (If not using banana leaves, wrap the pork in aluminum foil.) Bake on low until it comes apart easily when tugged with a fork, 3½ to 4 hours. Remove from the heat and allow the pork to cool enough before handling. With your hands or a fork, shred it into ¼-inch-thick strips and trim away any excess fat.

Before serving, heat the remaining achiote marinade and pour over the pork. Season with salt and pepper to taste. Place the *cochinita pibil* on a large serving platter with the iceberg lettuce leaves on the side. Spoon the pork onto the lettuce leaves and top with sour cream, if desired, salsa cruda or verde, and pickled onions. Wrap the lettuce leaf as if it were a flour tortilla.

REHYDRATING DRIED CHILE PEPPERS

Store bags of dried chiles away from direct sunlight until ready to use. If you are working with very hot chiles, you may want to handle them with latex gloves. Core and shake out the seeds. Then place the chiles in a bowl, add enough hot water to cover, and seal the bowl with plastic wrap to produce steam. The pepper will soften and be ready to use after 15 to 20 minutes. Do not oversoak. If called for, devein the chiles by removing their stringy inner ribs.

PUMPKIN BLOSSOM chicken

WHILE OUR GUEST GERARDO SUTER nourishes Mexico with his photographs that capture the country's cultural zeitgeist, his wife, Gerda, nourishes her family's and friends' appetites with her artistic interpretations of local ingredients. In this dish, chicken breasts are dressed up in nature's own spring couture: pumpkin blossoms.

Native to the Americas, pumpkin blossoms are the delicate flower of the big orange pumpkin, or *calabaza,* as it's called in Mexico. Once picked, the delicate, sweet-tasting blossoms last only a day or two. Popular in Mexican and Italian cuisine, pumpkin blossoms and zucchini blossoms can be found in farmers' markets from late spring through early fall.

If they're out of season, forgo the blossoms and wrap the chicken breasts in frozen spinach leaves, which will have a much stronger flavor but will still look lovely. Use a 6-ounce bag of frozen baby spinach leaves. Thaw, rinse, and pat the leaves dry before wrapping the chicken. For this get-together, Gerda garnished the chicken dish with tomatillos and shiitake mushrooms.

Serves 8.

8 skinless, boneless chicken breasts,
    pounded thin
Salt and fresh ground black pepper
8 ounces fresh goat cheese
Extra virgin olive oil
20 to 30 pumpkin or zucchini blossoms,
    cut into 4- to 5-inch strips
Eight 8 × 8-inch pieces aluminum foil

Preheat the oven to 375°F.

Season the chicken breasts with salt and pepper. Add roughly 1 tablespoon of cheese to one long chicken edge and spread evenly in a straight line. Carefully roll the chicken breast into a cigar shape, starting with the goat cheese edge. Using your fingers, dab the chicken roll with olive oil and then arrange overlapping pumpkin blossom strips on the outside of the chicken roll. Wrap each chicken roll in an aluminum sheet, making sure the ends are secure so that the goat cheese does not leak out.

Repeat with the remaining chicken breasts. Place them on a baking sheet and bake for 30 minutes. Spoon warm mole sauce (page 108) onto a large serving plate. After 30 minutes, remove the foil and arrange the breasts on a platter. Serve with extra mole sauce on the side.

RED mole

MOLES, WITH THEIR AZTEC ORIGINS, are sauces made from chiles and other ingredients, such as nuts, dried fruit, and chocolate. There are many mole recipes, and some have over twenty ingredients in them. Many Mexican families use recipes that have been passed down through the generations.

This is my interpretation of Gerda's mole sauce. Its numerous flavors—and three distinct chiles—vie for palate recognition. The moderately hot guajillo pepper lends this sauce its deep reddish-brown hue; the pasilla chile, which is actually a dried black chilaca chile, is a standard in many mole sauces; and the relatively mild ancho chile is actually a dried poblano pepper and gives a sweet, earthy taste. While this sauce has a kick to it, you can easily tone down the spiciness the same way the Aztecs did: add a couple extra squares of dark chocolate.

While at our party the mole was paired with chicken, it is also delicious on fancier fowl, such as Cornish hen, duck, or squab. My all-time favorite is mole spooned over simple white rice.

As you toast the dried chiles, the fumes may tickle or itch your throat, but this sensation will subside soon. You may want to use latex gloves when handling hot chiles.

This mole sauce may be stored in the refrigerator for up to a week. When reheating, lightly oil a skillet over medium heat, add the mole and as much chicken broth as needed to reconstitute the sauce.

This will make 3½ cups.

5 dried guajillo chiles, cored and seeded
5 dried pasilla chiles, cored and seeded
5 dried ancho chiles, cored and seeded
Extra virgin olive oil
4 large, ripe plum tomatoes, roughly chopped
½ Spanish onion, roughly chopped
4 garlic cloves, quartered
1 cup raisins
½ teaspoon cumin
½ teaspoon oregano
½ teaspoon thyme
½ teaspoon marjoram
1 tablespoon black peppercorns
¼ teaspoon cinnamon
4 whole cloves
½ to ¾ cup low-sodium chicken stock
1 tablespoon salt, plus more to taste
1 tablespoon sesame oil or olive oil,
    plus more as needed
1 ounce dark chocolate, such as Lindt

Loosely tear the dried chiles, making sure to discard any remaining seeds. In a heavy skillet, toast all 15 chiles in batches over moderate heat until they release their aroma, 15 to 20 seconds. Take care not to burn them.

Rehydrate (see page 105) and devein the chiles. Set aside.

Meanwhile, lightly coat the same skillet with olive oil and sauté the tomatoes, onion, garlic, and raisins until the skins of the tomatoes begin to peel off and the onion softens, about 5 minutes.

In a smaller pan, heat the dried herbs and spices until they release their aromas, less than a minute.

Place the rehydrated chiles, cooked vegetables, spices, ½ cup chicken stock, and salt into a food processor or blender. Puree the mixture until it is smooth. Strain the mole through a medium-mesh sieve.

Heat the tablespoon of sesame oil or olive oil in a skillet. Add the mole sauce and stir in the chocolate. When the chocolate melts, add more chicken broth if a thinner consistency is desired. Adjust salt to taste. Serve warm.

PICKLING ONIONS MELLOWS THEIR FLAVOR, turning them into a distinct condiment for serving with *cochinita pibil,* chicken, meat, or fish. These onions may be stored in the refrigerator for up to two weeks.

This will make about 2½ cups.

1½ cups red wine vinegar
2 tablespoons sugar
Dash of hot pepper sauce
Salt to taste
2 large red onions, peeled and thinly sliced

Combine all the pickling ingredients with 1½ cups water. Add the onions and store in a glass jar or container with a lid. Refrigerate for at least 4 hours before serving.

PICKLED onions

CHORIZO and beans

THIS IS NOT YOUR MOTHER'S PORK AND BEANS—it's my mother's. She and I came up with it one afternoon in 1992 just days after Hurricane Andrew ripped through our home in Miami. Looking around the kitchen, we found cans of cannelli (also called alubia) beans, chorizo, and beer.

With the electricity down, we cooked everything outside in our *paellera,* a gigantic outdoor skillet that runs on gas and is used for making paella. The result was this homey dish. Sometimes I double the recipe and use leftovers to make a buttery bean dip for bread, chips, or crackers. For the dip: Let the beans cool, pour them into a food processor with a little bit of olive oil, and puree until smooth.

Chorizo is a Spanish sausage cured with garlic and paprika. Mexican chorizo is slightly spicier. Either is widely available in most supermarkets and specialty stores.

Serves 8.

30 thin slices Spanish or Mexican chorizo,
    casings removed (about half a 9.5-ounce
    sausage)
Two 15-ounce cans white cannelli beans,
    drained and rinsed under cold water
½ cup beer
½ cup low-sodium vegetable or chicken stock
1 rosemary sprig or 2 teaspoons dried
    rosemary, plus 6 sprigs (optional),
    for garnish
Salt and freshly ground black pepper to taste

Halve the chorizo slices. In a pan sauté them for 2 to 3 minutes over medium-high heat. Over low-medium, add the beans and cook for a minute. Add the beer, stock, and one rosemary sprig, simmering until most of the liquid evaporates and the beans soften, about 5 minutes. Add salt and pepper to taste and garnish with remaining rosemary sprigs, if desired.

Three Milks Cake

TRES leches

THIS FESTIVE NICARAGUAN DESSERT, though enjoyed in other parts of Central America, is the first cake my mother taught me how to bake. I have since put my own signature on it by adding pecans and a liqueur, such as Chambord (black raspberry), or Baileys Irish Cream to the cake batter.

While this cake needs no fancy garnishes, I like to add fresh raspberries if I've used Chambord; or ribbons of dulce de leche (page 46) when paired with Baileys. My sister has nicknamed the one with dulce de leche as *quatro leches*, or "four milks cake."

This dessert tastes best when it is made a day ahead and served chilled.

It will make enough for 10 to 12 servings.

CAKE

Butter for greasing the pan
2 cups all-purpose flour
2½ teaspoons baking powder
5 large eggs, separated
2 cups sugar
¼ cup pecans, finely chopped
½ cup whole milk
3 tablespoons Chambord or Baileys Irish
   Cream
1 teaspoon vanilla extract

CREAM

One 12-ounce can evaporated milk
One 14-ounce can sweetened condensed milk
1 cup heavy cream

MERINGUE TOPPING

¾ cup sugar
3 egg whites

Preheat the oven to 350°F. Lightly butter a 9 × 13-inch baking pan. Sift the flour and baking powder together in a large bowl. Set aside.

In a mixing bowl, beat the egg whites on low-medium speed until soft peaks form. Slowly add the sugar and increase speed to medium-high until stiff peaks form. Then beat in one egg yolk at a time, incorporating each egg yolk for about 15 seconds before adding in the next one. Add the pecans. Slowly add half the flour, the milk, and then the remaining flour, liqueur, and vanilla. Occasionally scrape the sides of the mixing bowl. Keep mixing the cake batter until it is smooth and forms ribbons, for about 2 more minutes.

Pour the batter into the prepared pan. Bake for about an hour, or until the cake is golden and springy, and a toothpick inserted in the center comes out clean.

Cool in the pan on a rack for 10 to 15 minutes.

Meanwhile, make the cream by whisking together the evaporated milk, condensed milk, and heavy cream. Pierce the cake all over with the tines of a fork, and, while the cake is still warm, pour the cream evenly all over. Cool to room temperature.

To make the meringue topping, combine the sugar and 3 tablespoons water in a small saucepan and stir until the sugar dissolves. Bring to a boil and then simmer the sugar syrup until it reaches the "soft-ball stage" or 240°F on a candy thermometer, about 5 minutes.

At the same time that the sugar syrup comes to a boil, begin beating the egg whites on medium-high until they reach the soft-peak stage. Slowly pour in the sugar syrup along the sides of the mixing bowl and beat on low speed. When the sugar syrup has been incorporated, increase the mixing speed to medium and beat until stiff, glossy peaks form.

When the meringue topping has cooled slightly, spread it evenly on top of the cake with a spatula or knife. Refrigerate for at least 4 hours or overnight.

pumpkin blossoms

In Cuernavaca, the local farmers sell pumpkin blossoms on the side of the road. They pick bagfuls at sunrise and by midafternoon have sold out.

boquerones

These firm, white anchovies are sold in specialty delis and on the Web. Cured in a mixture of vinegar, brine, garlic, and lemon juice, they are a popular tapas dish in Spain. In Mexico we enjoyed them before our meal. It's customary to squeeze a few drops of lemon juice over them before eating.

no-fly zone

Natasha initially suspended pieces of the thorny nopal cacti to repel bats at her home in Acapulco. She liked the look, so she hung them at her home in Cuernavaca, too. Today Sully and Robert continue the tradition.

hallowed halls

Robert lent the Gelman Collection to the Parque Morelos Cultural Foundation, whose museum, Muros, opened in May 2004 in Cuernavaca's city center. There is a wing dedicated to Frida Kahlo and another showcasing murals. Many works feature Jacques' wife, Natasha. Jacques made a name for himself as a movie producer during Mexico's golden age of film. His work helped launch the career of Mario Moreno, also known as Cantinflas, one of the world's greatest comic actors.

dip dish

Cornhusks are typically used to make tamales and can be bought for a few dollars a bundle in the Latin section of your grocery store. We like to use them as dip holders when we entertain, to add another Latin touch to the setting. Bend the individual husks into the shape of a boat hull. Tie off the edges with string, raffia, or a piece of another husk.

salt mine

For a unique margarita presentation, rim your glasses with a colored salt instead of regular table salt. Peruvian pink salt, Hawaiian red salt, or Black Lava sea salt are all different kinds of salts that are available at many grocery stores and online. The salts pretty much all taste the same, but some are coarser than regular table salt, so before rimming your glasses, you might want to grind them for a minute with a mortar and pestle or with the back of a knife on your cutting board, just to make the granules a bit smaller. We rimmed our Szechwan Margaritas with Peruvian pink salt.

party accents

Traditional Mexican paper flowers are often associated with the festivities surrounding the Day of the Dead, but they make for bright table accents any time of year. Their flexible stems bend and work well as napkin holders. I found these at a craft store in Atlanta, but they are also available from many online sources. I keep some in my apartment for last-minute entertaining when I don't have time to run out to the store to buy fresh-cut flowers.

For place cards, we used *lotería* cards from a traditional Mexican children's bingo-like game. As place-card holders, they make for a fun guessing game for all ages. I bought these at a Mexican store in New York City called La Sirena, but they are easy to find online. With the remaining cards, I made refrigerator magnets by gluing small magnets onto the back of each card.

garden fresh

Sully and Robert's backyard overflows with native orchids, birds of paradise, and gardenias. For our table's centerpiece, we picked some roses and hibiscus to float in a large Mexican bowl. At night, a variety of jasmine, the *galán de noche* ("suitor of the night"), emits a sweet perfume from their garden. My grandmother used to have *galán de noche* on her porch and would tell me stories of how the nighttime aroma was known for its powers of seduction.

temazcal treat

For those who haven't experienced an Aztec Temazcal, it's similar to a Native American sweat lodge ceremony, except with roots in Aztec purifying practices. I first learned about it when I visited my sister. Mom wouldn't let me try it despite my pleas that it would "align my spirit with Mother Earth." She told me to "go roll around outside if you want to be close to nature." So imagine how excited I was when I found out that our Cuernavaca hotel, the Hosteria and Spa Las Quintas, had one. For about an hour you sit in a tiny, rocklike igloo, soaking up the heat of smoldering volcanic rock while inhaling herbal aromatics. It's a relaxing, enchanting experience.

is that my drink?

Colorful papier-mâché art has long been popular in Mexico. We turned these papier-mâché pendants into drink markers by looping them onto small pieces of thin, bendable wire from a hardware store. The mermaid is an image from a *lotería* card, while the Virgin of Guadalupe is Mexico's beloved patron saint.

BEATS

From classic mariachi to Grammy-winning rock, political anthems, and songs of love, we covered much of the Mexican musical spectrum at our lunch. We also gave a respectful nod to neighboring Guatemala with the sexy songs of Ricardo Arjona.

Histórico Banda el Recodo en Vivo
México en la Piel Luis Miguel
Border (La Linea) Lila Downs
Solo Ricardo Arjona
MTV Unplugged Maná

the heat in
the hamptons

THE HAMPTONS ARE LOCATED ON THE SOUTH FORK AT THE TIP OF LONG ISLAND, A SHORT DRIVE OR JITNEY RIDE FROM NEW YORK CITY. WITH THEIR MANICURED LAWNS, SAND DUNES,

and indigo seas, the Hamptons provide a rustic refuge from the hurly-burly of the big city. Isabel and I decided to set our barbecue here, at the home of our friend, fashion designer Carmen Marc Valvo.

Carmen spends the week in his skyscraping Manhattan atelier, but on weekends he and his partner, Christian Knaust, unwind in their Hamptons' cottage overlooking Mecox Bay. Far from the din of the runway, they love to entertain in the country. One summer weekend we gathered some mutual city friends for a grilling feast.

Whether it's a whole roasted pig on a spit in Puerto Rico or cured sausages over a charcoal grill in Uruguay, Latin Americans have long had a love affair with food cooked over fire. Oddly enough, it wasn't until I moved to the confines of Manhattan that I started grilling. When I was growing up, no one but my father or uncles were allowed to tend the grill. Women stayed in the kitchen making the gazpacho and handing the men plates of marinated meat. We didn't dare put them on the glowing embers! When I married, it was my husband who took charge of the "mysterious grilling work."

But during the course of writing this book, I was set on bringing equality to the grill. I bought a small gas grill and placed it outside on my tiny Manhattan terrace. Under my husband's tutelage, I began grilling away. I then tried my hand at charcoal and electric grills, stepping on a few male egos along the way, but was quickly forgiven when emerging with a plate of guava barbecue pork and chipotle corn.

No matter what kind of grill you have—gas, electric, or charcoal—the secret is learning how to harness the heat. Throwing a barbecue party, complete with cool drinks and garden decor, is the perfect way to start.

THIS IS A TRADITIONAL CUBAN DRINK THAT PEOPLE SERVE AT HOME, usually at afternoon summer parties. Some prefer it with 7UP or Sprite, and drink it like a shandy (called *clara* in Spain), but I like it without too many bubbles. We also prefer light beers that don't mask the flavor of the sugar and limes.

10 limes, quartered
⅔ cup superfine sugar
6 bottles light beer, chilled

Mash the limes and sugar in the base of a large pitcher. If you don't have a muddler, use a large wooden spoon, or just squeeze the limes to release the juice and toss in a few of the spent shells, then stir in the sugar. Add the beer and stir. Serve in frosted beer mugs.

BUL

SERVES 6

CARMEN colada

SERVES 8

SINCE CARMEN IS HALF SPANISH, HALF ITALIAN, we added amaretto to a traditional piña colada recipe in his honor. It makes the frothy drink even more decadent, a sweet treat after lunch when we all lounge by the water's edge. Add more ice for a thicker consistency and a higher yield.

3 cups pineapple juice
½ cup coconut cream, such as Coco Lopez
2½ cups light rum
½ cup coconut rum, such as Bacardi Coco
¼ cup amaretto, such as Amaretto di Saronno
6 cups ice
8 pineapple wedges

Mix all of the ingredients, except the ice and pineapple, in a blender. Add the ice and blend until pureed. Serve in tall glasses and garnish with the pineapple wedges.

YUGEÑO

SERVES 8

IF YOU LIKE SCREWDRIVERS, try this Latin version, which calls for the grape brandy Pisco, instead of vodka. It comes from Bolivia, where presumably it takes its name from the Yungas region.

5 cups orange juice
3 cups Pisco
8 orange slices

Pour the juice and Pisco into a pitcher. Serve in a tall glass filled with ice. Garnish the glasses with orange slices.

WHEN THE SUN SIZZLES, nothing satisfies like a cold cup of gazpacho. This deep salmon-colored, sweet, but slightly tart vegetable soup is my favorite heat remedy. The word *gazpacho*, according to the culinary encyclopedia *Larousse Gastronomique*, comes from the Arabic, meaning "soaked bread." Historians believe the first gazpacho was a Moorish introduction. It was made from bread, ground almonds, garlic, olive oil, and vinegar. With its origins in southern Spain's Andalusia, gazpacho was a way for peasants to stretch their day-old bread into a meal by softening it with olive oil and ripe vegetables. Tomatoes were introduced into the mix only after Columbus brought them back from the Americas in the fifteenth century. Today the "red," or tomato-based, gazpacho is the most popular in Spain. I first tasted this ubiquitous summer soup as a teenager while visiting my tía Anita in Madrid. This is her recipe.

It may be made up to two days ahead and refrigerated in a large bowl or pitcher. Making it ahead not only saves time but allows the flavors to blend. If ripe tomatoes are not in season or plentiful, use canned or a mixture of the two. Stir well before serving.

This recipe will make 8 servings.

GAZPACHO ANDALUZ

Extra virgin olive oil
1 red bell pepper, cored and seeded,
    roughly chopped
1 medium sweet onion, such as Vidalia,
    quartered
10 ripe plum tomatoes (fresh or canned),
    roughly chopped
1 cup tomato juice, or a tomato juice blend
    such as V8
2 plump cucumbers, peeled, seeded,
    and roughly chopped
1 to 2 medium garlic cloves, peeled
    and mashed
1 slice day-old baguette or white bread
    (about 1 ounce)
¼ cup sherry vinegar or red wine vinegar
1 tablespoon freshly squeezed
    lemon juice
2 teaspoons kosher salt
Freshly ground black pepper to taste
Thinly sliced chives or grilled croutons
    (recipe follows), for garnish

Coat a skillet with the olive oil, and heat. Over moderate heat, sauté the pepper and onion until they soften slightly, about a minute. Place them in a blender or food processor, along with the tomatoes, tomato juice, cucumbers, garlic, and baguette. If everything doesn't fit, do this in batches.

Puree the vegetables until liquefied. While the processor is running, drizzle in ½ to ¾ cup olive oil and the vinegar.

Strain the gazpacho into a large bowl through a medium-mesh sieve or a chinoise. This traps any remaining seeds or tough skins. Using your hands, squeeze the leftover pulp over the sieve to release as much liquid as possible. Stir in the lemon juice, kosher salt, and pepper to taste.

Serve chilled in bowls or cups. Garnish with chives or grilled croutons.

grilled croutons

½ baguette
2 tablespoons butter, melted
2 teaspoons chopped fresh parsley or chives

Thinly slice the baguette. Brush with the melted butter. Grill over medium heat until lightly charred, or bake in a 350°F oven until crisp and golden, about 12 minutes. Sprinkle with fresh parsley or chives. Place 1 to 2 croutons atop the gazpacho.

This will make 18 to 20 croutons.

BEEF SKEWERS WITH CHIMICHURRI sauce

CHIMICHURRI IS AN HERBACEOUS AND SLIGHTLY SPICY Argentine sauce that is used with beef, pork, and chicken. In Nicaragua a similar sauce accompanies *churrasco* (center-cut tenderloin) steaks. This recipe comes from my Argentine friend, Nestor Viton, whose uncle was a chef in Buenos Aires.

As for what cut of beef to purchase, use filet mignon (if you're feeling grand) or sirloin (less expensive).

This will make up to 20 skewers.

4 zucchini, sliced
2 large yellow squash, sliced
1 purple onion, halved, quartered,
    and separated
4 green peppers, diced
2 handfuls (about 12 ounces) cherry tomatoes
3½ pounds beef, cut into 2-inch cubes

Salt and freshly ground black pepper to taste
16 to 20 medium wooden skewers
    (8 inches long), soaked in water for
    at least an hour

Prepare the grill on medium-high heat.

Skewer alternating pieces of vegetables and meat, leaving enough "grabbing room" on either end of the skewers. Salt and pepper as desired. Lightly brush the skewers with about half the chimichurri sauce and line them up on the prepared grill. Cover and cook, turning occasionally, until the meat is at a desired doneness and the vegetables are lightly charred and tender, about 8 minutes for medium. Pour the remaining chimichurri sauce into one or two small bowls so that guests may add more, if desired.

chimichurri sauce

TO SAVE TIME, MAKE THE SAUCE IN ADVANCE. Store in the refrigerator up to two weeks. This recipe will make about 2 cups.

8 garlic cloves, minced
1 cup minced fresh, flat-leaf parsley
2 tablespoons fresh oregano, or 2 teaspoons
    dried
1 tablespoon red pepper flakes
¼ cup red wine vinegar
1 cup extra virgin olive oil
Salt and freshly ground black pepper to taste

Combine the first four ingredients in a bowl. With a fork, whisk in the red wine vinegar followed by the olive oil. Season to taste with salt and pepper. Set the mixture aside for at least 4 hours so that the flavors combine.

Grilled Green Spring Onions

CEBOLLITAS

WHILE VISITING HER SISTER IN MEXICO CITY, Isabel saw street merchants hawking baskets of grilled green onions, or *cebollitas*, which were eaten as a midday snack. They are readily available in spring and summer. Look for onions with large bulbs and hearty green tops. Trim the root ends and a couple inches off the tops. If green onions are out of season, scallions—which have much smaller bulbs—may be substituted, although since they are smaller, you will want to grill at least 25 of them.

These may be grilled ahead and served at room temperature in pretty breadbaskets.

16 large green onions, washed, trimmed,
    and patted dry
Kosher salt
Limes

Prepare the grill on medium-high heat. Grill the onions, covered, turning them a couple of times or more. They will be ready when the green parts dry out and start to char, and when the white parts have caramelized with a light golden hue. Remove from the heat. Before serving, sprinkle the onions with salt and squeeze on fresh lime juice.

THIS IS A MEXICAN TWIST ON THE TRADITIONAL CORN ON THE COB. Chipotles are ripe, smoked jalapeño peppers and are sold either dried or canned—usually in a spicy adobo sauce. If buying them canned, make sure to rinse off the sauce under cold water, to squeeze out the seeds, and to pat the chipotles dry on paper towels before mincing. The chipotle butter is also great on toasted bread.

8 ears fresh corn, husks on
2 dried or canned chipotle chile peppers,
    cored and seeded
4 tablespoons unsalted butter, softened
Kosher salt to taste

Soak the corn in water for 30 minutes.

If using dried chiles, rehydrate (see page 105). Finely mince the chiles and stir into the butter. Add a pinch of salt.

Over medium heat, grill the corn—husks on—for about 20 minutes, covered. Remove from the heat, peel off the husks, and brush with half the flavored butter. Grill for a few more minutes, turning occasionally, until cooked through. Remove from the grill, add salt to taste, and if more heat is desired, brush on the remaining butter. Serve warm.

CORN WITH chipotle butter

SUPER BOWL SUNDAY AT DR. FELIX GONZÁLEZ'S HOUSE always includes platefuls of juicy, grilled pork tenderloin medallions slathered in guava barbecue sauce. This Miami Cuban has been making his own fruity yet piquant sauce for years, which I have adapted here.

Unlike beef, pork should not be eaten rare, but rather medium to medium-well. If you have a meat thermometer, the internal temperature should reach at least 155°F for medium. The pork should marinate overnight, or at least for 4 hours before grilling.

The guava sauce may be made ahead and refrigerated for up to a week. Guava paste is widely available in Latin markets and through specialty retailers. Quince paste makes a good substitute.

This recipe makes about 2½ cups of sauce.

guava barbecue sauce

12 ounces guava paste, cut into small cubes
¼ cup red wine
½ cup freshly squeezed orange juice
¼ cup freshly squeezed lime juice
2 tablespoons Dijon mustard
2 garlic cloves, minced
4 tablespoons honey
1 teaspoon kosher salt

PORK tenderloin
WITH GUAVA BARBECUE SAUCE

In a small saucepan, combine all the sauce ingredients. Simmer over low heat, stirring occasionally with a wooden spoon until the guava paste dissolves and the ingredients combine to form a thick, syrupy sauce, 15 to 20 minutes. Cool to room temperature. If not using immediately, refrigerate.

3 pork tenderloins (1 to 1½ pounds each)
½ bottle red wine
½ cup balsamic vinegar
6 garlic cloves, peeled
Olive oil or vegetable oil for grilling

Marinate the pork overnight in the wine, balsamic vinegar, and garlic.

Preheat the grill on high. When hot, brush the pork tenderloins with the olive oil and sear each side for about a minute. Lower the heat to medium and cook covered for 8 to 10 minutes per side, brushing generously with the guava barbecue sauce at least twice.

Remove the pork tenderloins from the heat, glaze with another thick coat of the barbecue sauce, and rest on a plate for at least 5 minutes. Then slice the tenderloins into 3-inch medallions. The pork should be served warm with a side of papaya salsa.

papaya salsa

THIS SALSA MAY BE MADE UP TO A DAY AHEAD. It may be served chilled or at room temperature.

This makes about 3 cups of salsa.

2 cups papaya, cubed in ½-inch squares
1 Hass avocado, cut into small pieces
2 tablespoons diagonally sliced scallions
¼ cup lemon juice
Pinch of sugar
Pinch of salt

Combine all the ingredients together in a medium bowl. Toss, cover, and refrigerate.

BRANDED PINEAPPLE wheels with vanilla ice cream and caramelized walnuts

PINEAPPLE, ANOTHER NEW WORLD FRUIT, is available year round, though peak season is from March to June. When choosing a pineapple, look for fruit that is heavy for its size, has a pleasant aroma, bright green leaves that come off with a forceful twist, and flat eyes that are almost hollow. If you don't want to peel and core your own fruit, most large grocery stores sell peeled, cored, and sliced ripe pineapples.

Grilled pineapple slices are delicious on their own. Cook them before guests arrive, and then set the fruit aside, covered, at room temperature. If you're feeling indulgent—as we were—serve warm with a side of vanilla ice cream and caramelized walnuts.

This will serve 8.

1 whole ripe pineapple, peeled and cored
Vanilla ice cream
Caramelized walnuts (optional)

Prepare the grill on medium-low heat. Slice the pineapple into ¾-inch rounds. Over low-medium heat, grill for approximately 3½ minutes on each side, or until they become pliable.

Arrange two slices on each serving plate. Add a scoop of vanilla ice cream and a couple of caramelized walnuts, if desired.

caramelized walnuts

MAKE AHEAD AND KEEP IN AN AIRTIGHT CONTAINER FOR UP TO TWO WEEKS.

½ cup sugar
16 shelled walnuts

Line a baking sheet with parchment paper.

Pour the sugar into a small saucepan and cook over medium heat, stirring. When the sugar turns a caramel color, drop in the nuts two at a time, turn them with a fork to coat, and then use tongs or another fork to remove them. Place them on a lined baking sheet to cool.

greenhouse

Whenever you see a floral print on one of Carmen's dresses, you can bet the inspiration came from his backyard. In addition to perennials and annuals, he has water, shadow, and orchid gardens. When we set the table, he picked some newly bloomed hydrangeas. We tied them to the chairbacks and tucked them into the napkin holders.

ocean oasis

With the ocean within a short walking distance, Carmen and Christian's cottage home brims with charming marine themes, such as baskets filled with shells. To complement their aquamarine dishes, we replaced their traditional salt and pepper shakers with an array of handpicked seashells that we filled with salt and pepper. You can also find inexpensive seashells at craft stores.

well labeled

We like to give unique gifts to our hosts and hostesses, and while a bottle of wine isn't such a big deal, it's special when the wine is also the name of your host. So, for Carmen's party we picked up a few bottles of Carmen wine, which comes from one of the oldest and largest wineries in Chile, located in the foothills of the Andes. Other companies offer personalization services for wine bottles and labels. Also, some small wineries will personalize your wine for you when you order a case of twelve bottles.

BEATS

For our summer barbecue, we played laid-back tunes mixed with some toe-tapping rhythms. Putumayo's Latin-groove compilation includes songs by Funkanzazenji (mixing flamenco guitar with bass) and the smooth beats of El Conjunto Massalia. Columbian Juanes' fiery rock blended into the country-pop tunes of Bacilos, while Panamanian icon Rubén Blades and Colombian Carlos Vives infused a folksy feel into the afternoon.

Putumayo Presents Latin Groove
Mi Sangre   Juanes
Caraluna   Bacilos
Buscando América   Rubén Blades y Seis de
   Solar
El Amor de Mi Tierra   Carlos Vives

alta

cocina

A FASHIONABLE FEAST FOR 6

MAYBE

that we stayed up late to watch as kids. It could have been the fancy outfits our moms bought us every year for Nochebuena; to this day I can't eat Spanish *turrón* without thinking about velvet party dresses. But, more likely, it was the copious amounts of baby eau de toilette (Agustín Reyes Royal Violets, thank you very much) doused on us for the first seven years of our lives that altered our brain chemistry. Something—all of these things?—turned Carolina and me into aspiring glamour hounds, afflicted with a boundless love for high fashion, seductive scents, and fine food. Don't be mistaken, we didn't lead indulgent lives. After all, both our families immigrated to the United States with not much more than memories and hope for a better future. Without silver spoons, our mothers, in their own creative and resourceful ways, tried to teach us about the good things in life. As a result, we appreciate and, to be sure, act like giddy little girls when we find ourselves dressed up and seated before a delicacy.

New York is just the place to indulge in these kinds of experiences, especially during the ultimate homage to all things apparel: fashion week, where socialites, international glitterati, and artists collide. Donning our chicest gear and reporter passes, we hit show after show, taking in all the beautiful dresses, gorgeous models, and over-the-top attendees. With our sartorial hunger fully sated, we'll indulge in a meal at a trendy eatery or throw an impromptu celebration at one of our apartments.

So at the end of the most recent fall fashion week, we converged at the home of friend and fellow Venezuelan expat, designer Angel Sanchez, to celebrate his collection. Carolina and Angel met at a party and bonded over some of their favorite Venezuelan memories, including the beautiful women who win many Miss Universe titles; the way Venezuelans always dressed glamorously and how that inspired Angel's career; and, of course, traditional foods like *Bien Me Sabe,* a tiramisù-like dessert, which means "tastes good to me," and Tisana, a fruity punch that Venezuelan children enjoy at birthday parties. For this get-together, we supplied the elegant fare, including an adult version of Tisana and our Lovely Lobster Salad. Angel loaned us a couple of luxurious dresses and invited one stunning Argentine supermodel-friend, Ines Rivero. For our part, Carolina and I hit the city markets to unearth the truffle of Mexico—huitlacoche—for a sublime soup and to pick up table dressings, such as striking red dahlias. Keeping with this fashionable theme, I also decorated the place settings with pretty ribbon and fabric remnants. We toasted the night with oh-so-glamorous Latin Chic Cosmos and delighted in the oh-so-easy-to-make rum watermelon rubies.

THIS IS OUR SIGNATURE DRINK. We altered the traditional recipe by adding rich guava juice and replacing the orange liqueur with sweet raspberry liqueur. This drink is excellent over ice, too.

2 ounces cranberry juice
2 ounces guava juice
3 ounces citrus vodka, such as Grey Goose
    Le Citron
½ ounce raspberry liqueur, such as Chambord
Juice of 2 lime wedges

Combine all the ingredients in a shaker filled with ice. Shake and strain into chilled martini glasses.

LATIN CHIC COSMO
SERVES 2

THIS DIRTY MARTINI CALLS FOR FINO (DRY) SHERRY instead of vermouth. For the garnish, use manzanilla olives, which are everyday Spanish olives, with or without pimientos, but make sure they are pitted. You can also substitute olives stuffed with jalapeños or garlic. All of these can be found at most grocery stores.

1½ ounces dry sherry
6 ounces vodka or gin
1 tablespoon olive brine (or more, to taste)
6 large manzanilla olives

Combine all the ingredients, except the olives, in a shaker filled with ice. Shake and strain into chilled martini glasses and garnish each glass with 3 fat manzanilla olives.

DIRTY martini

SERVES 2

Martini Sucio

TISANA IS A GREAT PARTY DRINK. It's fruity and light, and traditionally served without alcohol at children's birthday celebrations in Venezuela. Carolina's mom serves this grown-up version in glasses festively garnished with star fruit at her New Year's parties. It's easy to make ahead of time, and it keeps refrigerated in a pitcher.

1 bottle dry white sparkling wine, such as cava
4 cups passion fruit juice
1 cup club soda
¼ to ⅓ cup sugar
1 small orange, sliced
1 small lemon, sliced
1 star fruit, sliced

In a punch bowl or pitcher, combine the wine, juice, soda, and sugar. Add the orange and lemon slices. Allow the mixture to steep in the refrigerator for at least an hour. Serve over ice. Garnish the glasses with the star fruit slices.

TISANA

SERVES 10

SIMPLE sangria

SERVES 8

WE'D BE REMISS IF WE DIDN'T INCLUDE SANGRIA, another traditional Latin fruit punch. With roots in Spain, it's generally made with red wine, oranges, lemons, cinnamon, and even brandy. My parents used to make huge batches of this citrusy version at their restaurant. I've cut the recipe down to a more manageable amount. You can also replace the wines with cava for a lighter, bubbly version.

2 cups orange juice
2 cups lemon juice
½ cup superfine sugar
½ bottle dry red wine
½ bottle dry white wine
1 orange, sliced
1 lemon, sliced
1 apple, cored and cut into thin wedges

In a large pitcher or punch bowl, combine the juices and the sugar. Stir the mixture until the sugar dissolves. Add both wines and stir. Add the orange and lemon slices and the apple wedges. Refrigerate to blend the flavors for at least an hour. Pour into goblets or red wineglasses over ice.

JOSEFINA's brandy alexander

SERVES 2

THIS WAS THE FAVORITE COCKTAIL of my paternal grandmother, Josefina González. It's more delectable than a regular Brandy Alexander because it calls for sweetened condensed milk instead of half-and-half. She and my mom had one every Saturday afternoon, but I like it better as an after-dinner treat.

2 teaspoons sweetened condensed milk
3 ounces evaporated milk
2 ounces dark crème de cacao
3 ounces brandy (preferably apricot)
Nutmeg

Combine the ingredients in a shaker filled with ice. Shake and strain into chilled martini glasses and garnish with a pinch of nutmeg.

• •

IN BARCELONA THEY MAKE THIS DRINK with equal parts sweetened condensed milk and espresso, and call it *biberón* ("baby's bottle"), but it's a little too rich for me. Espresso also tastes delicious with a dollop of coconut cream instead of milk. Try to serve it in a clear glass, because the espresso settles on top of the cream or milk for a pretty presentation. Pour on and enjoy!

1 tablespoon sweetened condensed milk
Demitasse of fresh-brewed espresso

Until-We-Meet-Tomorrow Coffee

CAFÉ hasta mañana

SERVES 1

IT'S OFTEN CALLED THE MEXICAN TRUFFLE. The black huitlacoche (pronounced *wee-la-CO-chay,* also spelled *cuitlacoche*) is a fungus that grows on corn. It has an opulent and woodsy taste that pairs well with cheese quesadillas, omelets, or buttered egg noodles. One of my favorite ways of showing off this earthy treasure is in a simple soup garnished with a crumbled salty cheese, such as Mexican cotija or feta, and half a pear tomato. In lieu of cheese, add a dollop of sour cream. Not only are your guests going to adore this soup, but its slate gray color packs a fashion punch.

Fresh huitlacoche can be difficult to find, but the canned variety is readily available in Mexican markets and online. This soup may be made a day ahead, refrigerated, and reheated before serving.

Serves 6 to 8.

HUITLACOCHE soup

1 tablespoon olive oil
1 tablespoon butter
3 garlic cloves, minced
½ medium onion, chopped
3 serrano chiles, cored, seeded, and chopped
Two 7.6-ounce cans huitlacoche
    (about 2 cups)
1 cup frozen sweet corn kernels,
    rinsed in cold water
2 cups low-sodium chicken stock
4 ripe plum tomatoes (fresh or canned),
    chopped
½ teaspoon (preferably Mexican) oregano
Pinch of cumin
Pinch of sugar
½ cup heavy cream
Salt and freshly ground black pepper to taste
3 ounces fresh crumbled cheese, for garnish
4 ounces sour cream (optional), for garnish
Palmful of pear tomatoes (optional),
    for garnish

Heat the oil and butter in a saucepan. When the butter melts, sauté the garlic, onion, and chiles over medium heat until the onion is soft. Stir in the huitlacoche and corn, and sauté for another 2 minutes. Stir in the stock, 1 cup water, tomatoes, oregano, cumin, sugar, and salt to taste. Bring the soup to a boil. Reduce the heat and simmer, half covered, for 20 minutes.

Mix in the cream and puree with a handheld immersion blender or food processor until smooth. Season with salt and pepper to taste. Garnish with cheese or sour cream and the pear tomatoes, if desired.

LOVELY lobster
salad

WHEN MY MOTHER WAS GROWING UP IN CARACAS, she remembers local fishmongers selling gigantic lobsters for very few bolivares. Every weekend, her mother would turn them into quotidian fare: boiled, steamed, grilled, or mixed in a salad. Imagine, eating lobster once a week!

Today a lobster meal is hardly inexpensive and is often reserved for elegant affairs. At this party, I reconstructed my grandmother's vintage lobster salad. No matter what the decade or the going rate is, this crustacean never falls out of fashion.

The dressing may be made up to a day in advance and simply whisked again before serving. As for the cucumbers and radishes, paper-thin slices are easily cut using a mandoline, but a sharp knife will do the trick. If you don't want to butcher your own lobsters, ask your fishmonger to split them lengthwise: 2 tails, 2 claws, and 2 knuckles. When buying passion fruit juice, make sure it is pure passion fruit juice and not a fruit blend.

This salad serves 6. The dressing makes 2½ cups.

DRESSING

2 cups passion fruit juice
Juice of 2 limes (about ⅛ cup)
⅛ cup sherry vinegar
Pinch of salt
2 tablespoons honey
⅛ cup walnut oil
⅛ cup vegetable oil

2 large garlic cloves, skins on
Extra virgin olive oil
3 lobsters (approximately 1.5 pounds each)
    cut into pieces
2 cucumbers, peeled and sliced into
    thin rounds
10 radishes, sliced into paper-thin rounds
1 mango, cut into small cubes
3 bunches watercress, trimmed and coarsely
    chopped

In a small saucepan, bring the passion fruit juice to a boil. Simmer until it reduces by half, about 20 minutes. Set aside to cool.

Pour the passion fruit reduction into a medium bowl and whisk in the lime juice, vinegar, salt, and honey. Drizzle in the walnut and vegetable oils while continuing to whisk until emulsified.

Skins on, mash the garlic with the wide portion of a chef's knife or meat mallet. Coat a large, heavy skillet with olive oil, and heat. When hot, add the garlic and lobster pieces (you will probably need to cook the lobster in two batches).

Cook the lobster, covered, over medium heat for about 4 minutes. Turn the lobster pieces over with a pair of tongs, cover, and cook for another 4 minutes or until done. The exposed meat should have golden streaks. Set aside on a plate and cover with aluminum foil. Discard the garlic.

Pour half of the dressing into a medium bowl and toss with the cucumbers, radishes, and mango. Add more salt, if desired.

Arrange a bed of watercress on each plate, drizzle about a spoonful of dressing over it, layer the cucumber-radish-mango mixture, and place the lobster pieces on top. Serve immediately.

SPAGHETTINI
WITH cilantro
pesto sauce

THIS IS A TRIBUTE TO MY ITALIAN FATHER, who was born in Parma, a city renowned for its cheese and ham. For this dish, Italian pesto gets a Latin makeover with cilantro and serrano peppers. Though traditionalists make pesto with a mortar and pestle to give it that rustic texture, I save time by making it in a food processor. The secret is to pulse the ingredients for mere seconds.

The sauce may be made ahead and refrigerated for up to a week, although the bright green hue of the cilantro will fade over time.

This makes 6 servings.

PESTO SAUCE

2 garlic cloves, halved
3 serrano peppers, cored, seeded, and
    quartered
2 cups tightly packed flat-leaf parsley leaves
2 cups tightly packed cilantro leaves
½ cup extra virgin olive oil, or more to taste
¼ cup dry white wine
¾ cup finely grated Parmesan cheese, plus
    more for sprinkling on top
1 cup roasted macadamia nuts
Salt and freshly ground black pepper to taste

1 pound spaghettini (thin spaghetti)

Place the garlic, serrano peppers, parsley, and cilantro in a food processor and pulse on and off for 10 seconds. Add the remaining pesto ingredients and pulse until mostly smooth, wiping the sides of the food processor with a spatula as needed.

In a large pot, boil the spaghettini in salted water according to the package directions, for about 6 minutes. When al dente, quickly drain the pasta (leaving it a bit wet) and toss it in a large bowl with the pesto sauce. Adjust the salt and pepper to taste and add more olive oil if needed. Serve immediately with grated Parmesan cheese.

WATERMELON RUBIES DRIZZLED WITH rum sauce

WHEN WE WERE LITTLE, my mother would hand my brother Christian and me each a melon baller and half a watermelon, and we'd pretend to be gem miners digging out "rubies." It was her way of getting us to help out in the kitchen.

This easy fruit salad should be made the day of your party, although the watermelon may be scooped up to six hours ahead and chilled. The sauce—which takes minutes to put together—should be made just before serving or else it will harden.

For a more artistic presentation, use a melon ball scooper with two different-sized heads.

This serves 6.

1 medium watermelon, preferably seedless
Juice of 1 lime

RUM SAUCE

½ cup sugar
½ cup dark rum
½ teaspoon ground cinnamon

Halve the watermelon lengthwise. Using a melon baller, carve out little round "rubies" and place them in a large bowl. Pour the lime juice over them, toss gently, cover with plastic wrap, and refrigerate until ready to serve.

To make the sauce, take a small saucepan and heat the sugar, rum, and cinnamon, stirring until the sugar just starts to dissolve (it should not dissolve completely) and small bubbles appear on the sides of the pan. Remove from the heat. Using a spoon, drizzle the sauce over the chilled watermelon rubies and serve in individual bowls. They may be eaten with a fork or fingers.

Tastes Good to Me

BIEN me sabe

THE QUINTESSENTIAL VENEZUELAN DESSERT, *bien me sabe* literally means "tastes good to me." It's believed to have originated in the convents of southern Spain, where the nuns flavored their pastry cream with almond milk. When the sisters arrived in the New World—Scriptures and recipes in tow—rich coconut milk was substituted for the almond milk.

The original family recipe is from my great-aunt Mercedes Camps, who once hid a young democrat (and future president of Venezuela) Rómulo Betancourt from the opposition dictatorial government. He lived in her house for three weeks, and family folklore has it, he told her that she made the best *bien me sabe* in all of Caracas. When Betancourt left her house, my great-aunt disguised him as a woman in one of her dresses.

Back then, women like my great-aunt made *bien me sabe* by squeezing the milk out of three whole coconuts. They used twelve egg yolks and baked their own ladyfingers. I've simplified my great-aunt's recipe to make it healthier and easier.

Unsweetened coconut milk is widely available in many grocery stores and in Asian markets. As for the ladyfingers, I buy the harder Italian ones, though soft ladyfingers may also be used.

Make this a day or two ahead, so that the ladyfingers have time to absorb the flavors.

This dessert will serve up to 10 guests.

24 ladyfingers (one 7-ounce package)
Sweet vermouth
Dark rum
3 tablespoons cornstarch
6 large egg yolks
Pinch of salt
Two 14-ounce cans unsweetened coconut milk
One 14-ounce can sweetened condensed milk
¼ teaspoon vanilla extract
Ground cinnamon

Line the ladyfingers atop a baking sheet or other flat surface. Covering the mouth of a vermouth bottle with your thumb, moisten—but do not drench—the ladyfingers with the alcohol. Flip them over and repeat on the other side with a bottle of rum.

Dissolve the cornstarch in 5 tablespoons of cold water. In a large mixing bowl, combine the egg yolks, dissolved cornstarch, and salt. Whisk until combined, and then set aside.

In a medium saucepan add the coconut milk, condensed milk, and vanilla. Over low heat, stir for about 5 minutes. The mixture should simmer lightly but not come to a boil. Remove about ¼ cup of the warm coconut mixture and stir into the egg yolks to temper them. Then pour the entire egg mixture into the saucepan, raise the heat to low-medium, and whisk constantly until the mixture begins to thicken.

The second the mixture thickens, remove it from the heat. This is very important: It will take only a minute or less to thicken. If it is left on the stovetop for more than a minute, the coconut cream will curdle and turn lumpy.

In a deep 8 × 8-inch baking dish, arrange a layer of ladyfingers (some will need to be broken in half so that they fit). Top with up to a 1-inch layer of the coconut cream. Add another layer of ladyfingers and the remaining cream. Smooth the top of the cake with a spatula. Chill overnight or for a couple of days.

When ready to serve, use a sifter to delicately dust the top of the cake with the cinnamon.

say cheese!

There are many Spanish and Latin American cheeses that you can serve at a dinner party to whet your guests' appetites. Here is a list of the ones we served, with a side of halved pear tomatoes, at Angel's home.

Garrotxa: semifirm goat cheese made in the Pyrenees, Catalonia

Mahon: a bold, semifirm cow's milk cheese aged in caves on the Balearic island of Minorca

Tetilla: a buttery cow's milk cheese from the province of Galicia in Spain (and, yes, as the name implies, it's shaped like a breast)

Irazu: white cow's milk cheese with tiny holes, named after the most revered volcano in Costa Rica

Queso de Mano: Venezuelan cow's milk cheese, stretched out by hand to give it a multilayered appearance

all shook up

Someone once brought me maracas from her Cancún vacation; the kind found at tourist traps—palm trees and the word "Cancún" prominently painted across the tops of them. I decided to spray paint them a metallic silver. It took all of five minutes to do and a few hours to dry. I display them by my stereo, and guests have a great time playing with them when grooving to the music.

latin lovelies

Florists have long relied on Latin American flowers and plants for their arrangements. For Angel's party, we bought dramatic red dahlias, which come from Mexico. Poinsettias also hail from Mexico, bougainvilleas are native to Brazil, and pretty and edible nasturtiums, which are sold in gourmet stores and can be used to adorn your lobster salad, come from Peru.

rock on

Here's a simple trick to add drama to your floral and candle arrangements: use rocks at the base of a glass vase. We filled a few shallow bowls and candle holders with tiny black rocks picked up at a craft store. After the party is over, store them for the next one.

table dressing

Sometimes a table is just too pretty to cover with a tablecloth. Angel's metallic table is one of those, so we made some cool place mats. Hardware stores sell sheets of Plexiglas, and they'll cut them to size. Clear or black Plexiglas, which we used for Angel's table, makes for a highly glossy look that is inexpensive, easy to clean, and long lasting.

sartorially speaking

I prefer fabric napkins to paper napkins, but store-bought cloth napkins can be expensive. Instead I head to a fabric store and buy a yard or two from a remnant roll. I cut out 10 × 10-inch squares and fray the edges with scissors. For this table setting, we rolled them up and tied them with thin strips of black silk ribbon, also from the fabric store. As a final fashion accent, we randomly scattered big sequins across the tabletop.

common scents

I joke with Carolina that we've been primping for parties since we were in diapers. Like their moms before them, our moms splashed us with either Agustín Reyes Royal Violet's eau de toilette, a brand originally made in Cuba, or Spain's Nenuco cologne. Both moms would pour a couple of drops on our heads and comb it into our hair so that we would smell nice. Sometimes, when we entertain, we'll leave bottles in the bathroom for guests to freshen up. It's a nice, sentimental Latin touch.

tempting turrones

Because it was once so hard to find in the States, *turrón,* a Spanish nougat generally made from almonds, egg whites, and honey, made appearances at our homes only on special occasions. Now you can easily find *turrones* online, in gourmet grocery stores, and in the ethnic sections of most grocery stores. El Lobo and 1880 are popular, quality Spanish brands. We gave some to Angel for his hospitality.

what's *¡hola!*?

Along with a few Spanish and international stars, *¡Hola!* magazine mostly dedicates its oversized pages to photographs of Spanish and European royalty—even their obscure distant relatives—lounging in their villas or cavorting on the Spanish star-studded island of Mallorca. *¡Hola!* takes us on weekly escapes to lavish, grandiose, and sometimes scandalous landscapes without leaving the house. Many newsstands in New York, Miami, Dallas, and Los Angeles carry the oversized magazine. Subscribe online at www.hola.com. Leave some copies on your coffee table to provide your guests with good star-gawking.

BEATS

We looked to runway-worthy beats to keep our style quotient at a high all night long. Two Latin compilations complemented the groovy sounds of multicultural Yerba Buena and Colombian duo Aterciopelados. While we ate dinner, classical guitarist supreme John Williams played Venezuelan waltzes. Then, as we cleared the plates, we got moving again to the funky and irreverent rockers Los Amigos Invisibles.

....

Barrio Latino I and *II*
President Alien   Yerba Buena
Gozo Poderoso   Aterciopelados
El Diablo Suelto   John Williams
The New Sound of the Venezuelan
   Gozadera   Los Amigos Invisibles

....

romance in

la romana:
un paso doble

A ROMANTIC DINNER FOR 2

I'VE LOVED BALLET SINCE THE AGE OF FIVE, WHEN I SLID MY FEET INTO THAT FIRST PAIR OF SOFT PINK SLIPPERS. AT TWELVE I WAS FITTED FOR MY FIRST PAIR OF POINTE SHOES. A LITTLE wobbly at first, I soon learned to balance on one leg while holding the other in arabesque. I studied flamenco in college with a teacher who made us swing broomsticks up and around our heads to build arm strength. When I moved to New York, my first job was teaching ballroom dancing—fox-trot, merengue, *paso doble*—to couples, many of whom were about to walk down the aisle.

So, when Herman Cornejo and Carmen Corella, two professional ballet dancers and dear friends, asked us to arrange an enchanted evening to celebrate their fifth anniversary, I was honored.

Years ago, in the suburbs of Buenos Aires, Herman's mother signed up her shy eight-year-old son for ice-skating lessons. But it was the sea of nimble bodies pirouetting to Tchaikovsky in his sister's ballet class that captivated Herman's imagination. The *maestro,* eager to acquire a boy to pair with his tutued sprites, convinced Herman to trade in his ice skates for ballet slippers. Miles away, Carmen was growing up in the outskirts of Madrid, following her brother into the ballet world, and later receiving international acclaim for her interpretation of the saucy Mercedes in *Don Quixote.*

Though oceans apart, Herman and Carmen eventually ended up dancing for the prestigious American Ballet Theatre in New York and living in the same apartment building. Like any great ballet story, the main characters don't always realize they are meant for each other. She was older, three inches taller (without pointe shoes on), and involved with another dancer. Then, during a tour in Japan, under the flickering lights of Tokyo's neon-bathed streets, Herman and Carmen shared their first kiss.

Ballet patrons J. Pepe and Emilia Fanjul graciously opened their Dominican Republic home in Casa de Campo so that we could host this intimate party. Isabel gathered local flowers, antique crystal, and candles to decorate their patio. Meanwhile, I prepared a light Caribbean dinner. Together we helped Carmen style her long black hair. When she walked out in a floor-length gown by Oscar de la Renta, Herman could not help but smile. Over dinner, the couple toasted with a glass of cava to another five years of bliss. Then Isabel and I said good-bye, allowing them to finish their dinner in private.

The next day, we went into the center of La Romana, looking to buy food and flowers for our husbands, who were flying in from New York, ready to spend a romantic evening with us. Yes, big parties are nice, but sometimes a *paso doble* ("two-step") is twice as nice.

AGUA DE valencia

SERVES 2

A MIMOSA WITH A LATIN TWIST, Agua de Valencia is made with cava, a light, crisp, and fruity sparkling white wine from northeastern Spain, near Barcelona, using classic Champagne methods. I first savored it in Valencia, a small coastal town south of Barcelona, where it is served at cafés and bars. We recommend using Freixenet and Segura Viudas cavas. You can also make this drink in pitcher-portion.

1 ounce orange liqueur, such as Cointreau
1 cup orange juice
Cava
2 orange slices

In two chilled champagne glasses, divide the Cointreau and juice. Stir to mix. Top each with cava and garnish with an orange slice.

DOMINICAN goddess

SERVES I

THIS DRINK IS SERVED AT BEACH BARS in the Dominican Republic. If you know any Dominicans, impress them by offering it at your next party.

2 ounces light rum
Grapefruit juice
Sprite or 7UP

Pour the rum into a tall glass filled with ice. Fill the glass with equal parts grapefruit juice and Sprite or 7UP.

To Die Dreaming

MORIR soñando

SERVES 8

IMAGINE DRINKING AN ORANGE CREAMSICLE. That's this drink. My Dominican friends tell me that their mothers and grandmothers would make them drink *morir soñando* as kids to "put some meat on their bones." It's nonalcoholic and easy to make in large batches for serving all week long. Some Dominicans make it with lemon and lime juice; others use whole milk or sweetened condensed milk. Just make sure that both the milk and the juice are extra cold to avoid curdling. For a tasty adult modification, add light or dark rum—dark for more flavor.

3 cups evaporated milk, chilled
½ cup superfine sugar
3 cups pulpless orange juice, chilled

In a pitcher, combine the milk and sugar, stirring until most of the sugar is dissolved. Add the juice and refrigerate until ready to serve. Pour into old-fashioned glasses filled with ice and serve.

THIS SALAD IS ONE OF COLORS AND CONTRASTS, melding green peppery arugula, orange candied mango, soft cheese, and crisp jicama. Set in purple radicchio leaves, it makes for a dramatic first act.

Jicama is a vegetable that when eaten raw tastes a bit like a water chestnut, with hints of tart apple and pear. Look for medium plump jicamas. If you lightly scratch one, the flesh should be juicy.

The dressing may be made up to two days ahead, refrigerated, and whisked together before serving.

This serves 2. The dressing recipe makes ¾ cup.

ARUGULA SALAD WITH MOZZARELLA AND GREEN MANGO jam

DRESSING

1 tablespoon honey
2 tablespoons balsamic vinegar
1 teaspoon salt, or more to taste
Freshly ground black pepper to taste
¼ cup extra virgin olive oil

½ jicama, peeled and cut into ½-inch-wide × 3-inch-long sticks (about 20)
2 handfuls arugula, washed and patted dry
2 radicchio cups (optional)
2 generous slices fresh mozzarella
2 spoonfuls green mango jam (page 47)

Using a fork, whisk together the first four dressing ingredients. Continue whisking while slowly drizzling in the olive oil.

Rinse the jicama sticks under cold water, pat dry, and set aside. Place the arugula in a bowl and toss with a couple of tablespoons of the dressing.

When ready to plate the salad, place the arugula in the radicchio cups, if using, or on the plate. Top with the jicama sticks, mozzarella, and a spoonful of the mango jam. Place the remaining salad dressing on the table for the guests to serve themselves.

CARIBBEAN lamb chops with tomato-cinnamon coulis

PHILIPPE MONGEREAU IS A CHARMING PARISIAN who, as executive chef for the resort Casa de Campo, oversees eight different restaurants. Before settling in the Dominican Republic, he worked as a chef in Paris, Versailles, Los Angeles, and Tokyo. Though Philippe makes yearly pilgrimages back to France, he says he's at home on this Caribbean island.

The Tomato-Cinnamon Coulis that forms a bed for the lamb chops is a preserve found in many Dominican homes, especially in the summer, when tomatoes are at their peak.

This serves 2. The coulis recipe makes about 2 cups.

½ cup fresh or dried breadcrumbs
2 tablespoons minced garlic
3 tablespoons finely chopped cilantro leaves
Vegetable or olive oil
1 rack of lamb (about 7 ribs), Frenched
Salt to taste
1 tablespoon Dijon mustard
2 cinnamon sticks (optional), for garnish
Tomato-Cinnamon Coulis (recipe follows)

Preheat the oven to 425°F.

In a food processor, combine the breadcrumbs, garlic, and cilantro, pulsing for a few seconds so that all the ingredients are well mixed together. Transfer to a large, flat plate.

Heat just enough oil to coat a large, ovenproof sauté pan. When hot, sear the lamb over high heat, starting with the fattiest side. Once it has browned, liberally sprinkle the rack with salt.

Brush a thin layer of the mustard over the outside of the rack and then dredge it with the flavored breadcrumbs.

Place the lamb rack in the sauté pan or a baking pan, fat side up, and place in the preheated oven. Cook until desired doneness (if cooking a small rack it will take 10 minutes for rare, 15 to 20 minutes for medium rare).

Remove the lamb from the oven and cover with a large piece of aluminum foil. Let it stand for 5 minutes. Then, using a sharp knife, cut between the bones to divide the chops. Spoon the warmed Tomato-Cinnamon Coulis on serving plates and place three to four lamb chops on each. Garnish with cinnamon stick, if desired.

tomato-cinnamon coulis

THIS COULIS, WHICH DOMINICANS CALL *MERMELADA DE TOMATE*, may be made days ahead, refrigerated, and warmed before serving. Store leftovers in the refrigerator for up to two weeks and use as a sandwich spread or as a dipping sauce for fried calamari.

6 medium ripe tomatoes
    (or 12 small ripe plum tomatoes)
2 tablespoons olive oil
2 tablespoons packed, light brown sugar
1 cinnamon stick
1 tablespoon salt, or more to taste
Freshly ground black pepper to taste
½ teaspoon sugar, or more to taste

Make a small incision on the bottom of the tomatoes. Immerse them in boiling water for 5 to 8 seconds, then in a bath of iced water. Peel the tomatoes, cut them in half, and, with the palm of your hand, gently squeeze them to remove the seeds.

In a large saucepan over medium heat, add the olive oil and brown sugar. Cook until it turns into a thick, caramel-like consistency, about 8 minutes, stirring constantly to avoid burning the sugar. Add the seeded tomatoes and cinnamon stick and cook over low-medium heat for about 1 hour and 15 minutes, allowing the tomatoes to release and cook in their natural juices. Adjust the heat to low, add the salt, pepper, and sugar, and cook covered for a half hour. Let cool.

Remove the cinnamon stick before serving. Add more salt and pepper, if desired.

TWO-TONE melon soup

IN THIS CHILLED FRUIT PUREE, the honeydew's sweetness is layered with soft hints of allspice and cream. Meanwhile, the cantaloupe is infused with lime and crisp chamomile tea leaves. The two fruit purees are then artfully combined.

This recipe may be made up to two days in advance and refrigerated. In the Dominican Republic, we served it to Herman and Carmen, and to our husbands the following evening.

This recipe makes 4 servings.

HONEYDEW CREAM

½ small honeydew (about 1 pound), cubed
2 tablespoons sugar
2 tablespoons heavy or light cream
¼ teaspoon allspice

CANTALOUPE SOUP

2 chamomile teabags
½ small cantaloupe (about 8 ounces), cubed
2 tablespoons lime juice
½ teaspoon maple syrup

In a food processor or blender, puree the honeydew cubes. Transfer the honeydew puree to a bowl. Whisk in the sugar, cream, and allspice. Cover and refrigerate.

Boil ½ cup water and steep 2 chamomile teabags for 5 to 7 minutes. Set aside.

In a food processor or blender, combine the cantaloupe cubes, lime juice, maple syrup, and the hot chamomile tea. For a smooth consistency, strain the cantaloupe puree. Place it in a bowl, cover, and chill along with the bowl of honeydew puree for at least an hour before serving.

When ready to serve, ladle the heavier honeydew puree on the bottom of a bowl and spoon the lighter cantaloupe puree in the center. You may also dispense the cantaloupe soup through a plastic squeeze bottle.

ESPRESSO suspiros

"*SUSPIRO*" IS THE SPANISH WORD FOR "SIGH." It's an excellent metaphor for these light-as-air meringues, which are sold in pastry shops all over Latin America and are often flavored with coffee, chocolate, or coconut. We like to dip them into a midafternoon cup of coffee or a glass of warm Andean milk (page 57).

The meringues may be stored in an airtight container for up to a month.

This recipe makes about 30 meringues.

½ cup sugar
1 teaspoon instant espresso or instant coffee
2 large egg whites, at room temperature
¼ teaspoon cream of tartar

Preheat the oven to 225°F. Line a large baking sheet with parchment paper.

In a small bowl, mix the sugar and espresso. Set aside.

Place the egg whites and cream of tartar in a mixing bowl. Beat the egg whites on low until they become frothy. Increase the mixer speed to high. When soft white peaks begin to form, add the sugar and espresso, a little at a time, scraping the sides of the mixing bowl as needed. Continue to beat until the meringue holds stiff, glossy peaks.

Using a pastry bag with a medium star tip, pipe out 2-inch-wide meringue florets onto the prepared baking sheet, leaving about ½ inch of space between each meringue. Bake for about 1 hour and 15 minutes. (Do not peek by opening the oven door, or you will let moisture in and end up with sticky *suspiros*!) Turn the oven off, and let the *suspiros* cool inside for another 20 minutes. They should easily slide off the parchment paper; if not, leave them in the oven for another 15 minutes.

a coterie of crystal

For a romantic table topper, we mixed and matched an assortment of vintage wineglasses that we bought at a New York City flea market. We used the glasses as vases to hold flowers that we picked from the property, including stunning white hibiscus. Then we centered the glasses on and around fresh-cut leaves and bougainvillea vines.

almond joy

For a tasty pre-dinner treat that also works as a place-card holder, fill an eggcup with fragrant toasted almonds and top with a homemade place-card. Like the wineglasses that we used as centerpieces, eggcups can be bought at flea markets or fine china shops.

To toast the almonds, preheat the oven to 350°F, spread the blanched nuts on a baking sheet, and toast them, shaking the sheet once or twice, until they start to turn golden brown, in 5 to 10 minutes. Place cards take just a few minutes to create and make the setting special. For these place cards, we cut a single stationery note card into small squares and with a gold marker wrote the word *"amor"*—"love"—instead of a name.

beany baby

An easy and inexpensive way to enhance the presentation of cookies, or, in this case, Carolina's espresso *suspiros,* is to serve them on a bed of shiny dark coffee beans. This won't work with caramel treats or anything syrupy, since the beans will cling. Place a mound of coffee beans on any plate, filling it so that just the rim of the plate is visible, and top the beans with your goodies. Use the beans for fresh roasted coffee or store in a plastic bag in the freezer for your next party.

coffee time

While the British are known for their teatime, Latinos can't live without a midday *cafecito,* a little espresso coffee, which generally follows lunch, or is the intermission between lunch and dinner. *Cafecito* is made with a cup of rich espresso, with or without sugar (and sometimes a splash of sweetened condensed milk or coconut cream), and a little sweet note, such as *suspiros,* a brioche, or a guava pastry.

Other ways to enjoy your *cafecito:*

Picardía	espresso with whiskey
Jerezano	espresso with sweet sherry (moscatel or cream)
Castellano	espresso with anisette liqueur, such as Marie Brizard
Carajillo	espresso with cognac

BEATS

Dominicans get their groove on with bachatas and merengues, two different music styles that originated on the island. Merengues are frenetically fast party beats, while bachatas are slower and often tell stories of love and heartbreak. Some Dominicans say that the reason merengues are called that is because it's the type of music the women making meringues listened to while feverishly beating eggs.

We're not sure if that's true, but considering the strength it takes to beat those eggs to perfection by hand, we bet the fast-paced music helps. For Carmen and Herman, we started the evening with romantic bachatas and then burned some energy with classic and new merengues. As the moon rose, we slowed it down again with Spanish crooner Alejandro Sanz, because, after all, this is a chapter of romance.

Bachata Rosa   Juan Luis Guerra y 4.40
We Broke the Rules   Aventura
Grandes Exitos   Sergio Vargas
Contra la Marea   Gisselle
MTV Unplugged (Live)   Alejandro Sanz

los angeles.

an oscar party in the hollywood hills

A CINEMATIC COCKTAIL GATHERING FOR 8

ALL RIGHT, SO OUR INVITATIONS TO THE OSCARS NEVER ARRIVED IN THE MAIL, BUT THAT'S NEVER STOPPED US FROM THROWING AN ACADEMY AWARDS BASH. ISABEL AND I HAVE MANY FRIENDS on the West Coast, so we decided to fly there for an Oscar weekend. We sent out old-movie postcards as invites to a cast of our closest L.A. friends.

Among them was Sami Hayek, a talented architect originally from Coatzacoalcos, Mexico, who had just completed a sitting room and outdoor deck in a house on Coldwater Canyon. It was the ideal setting. The cozy space had plush sofas, a giant plasma TV, and a sleek fireplace built from green onyx slabs.

When we got to Los Angeles, Isabel and I headed to the farmer's market on Fairfax and Third for culinary inspiration. After thinking up a menu of tempting drinks and tapas, we drove to the local public library in search of old Mexican movie classics starring the late, great María Félix.

As friends began to arrive, the sky was a spotless Technicolor blue. Sweet Matadoras were poured into champagne flutes while conversation flowed. Above us, on the television screen, Hollywood royalty traipsed down the red carpet in glittering gowns. Commenting on who was wearing what, we all got in touch with our inner fashion critic. By the time the chocolate flans were passed around, all bets had been placed on which movie would take home the coveted Best Picture award. When the show was over, our party was just beginning. We danced in tight quarters underneath the flickering black-and-white images of María Félix's film *Doña Bárbara*. As the clock struck midnight, Isabel passed around *Beso de Angel* nightcaps.

The next morning we made our way toward Olvera Street, the oldest in Los Angeles. There a lively Mexican market unfolds with stands selling everything from miniature guitars and silver jewelry from Taxco to giant sombreros. It also has restaurants, taco stands, and plenty of mariachi music. We shared a bag of decadent *churros* dripping with *cajeta* (see page 46) as a trio of musicians belted out *"Cielito Lindo,"* one of my favorite folk songs.

matadora

SERVES 2

BRIGHT RED GRENADINE TURNS THE traditional Mexican matador cocktail, a pineapple and tequila concoction, into a pretty, pink drink. So we added an "a" at the end of the word "matador" to reflect its feminization. Use a clear tequila, like silver tequila, so the fruit colors come through.

4 ounces pineapple juice
Juice of 1 lime
1 ounce grenadine
2 ounces tequila
2 pineapple wedges

Combine all the ingredients, except the pineapple wedges, in a shaker filled with ice. Shake and strain into champagne flutes. Garnish each glass with a pineapple wedge.

Torito

LITTLE bull

SERVES 8

THIS REFRESHING DRINK IS FROM Sami's mother and is one of his favorites. We served it to the raves of all the guests. Use fresh, ripe mangoes, but if they are not available, Goya sells frozen pulp. Add more ice for thicker consistency and a higher yield.

4 cups mango juice
Pulp of 1 ripe mango or 14-ounce package
    frozen mango pulp
2 cups light rum, such as Bacardi Superior
4 cups ice
8 mango wedges

Mix all the ingredients, except the ice and mango wedges, in a blender. Fill the blender with ice and blend until smooth. Serve in tall glasses and garnish with pieces of mango.

Kiss of an Angel

BESO de angel

SERVES I

KAHLÚA IS BEST SERVED COLD, and for this drink the milk should also be chilled so that it sits on top of the Kahlúa. Carolina and I first had this in Cuernavaca at Las Mañanitas, a picturesque outdoor restaurant overrun with gorgeous peacocks. Use clear shot glasses for this drink so that your guests can see the effect. This isn't a shooter; it's meant to be sipped slowly. Kahlúa also tastes great in coffee.

1 ounce Kahlúa
1 tablespoon evaporated milk

Pour the Kahlúa into the shot glass. Using a spoon, slowly drizzle the milk on top.

ROBERTO roy

SERVES I

THIS IS OUR TAKE ON the dry version of the honorific drink traditionally drunk to toast Scottish folk hero Rob Roy MacGregor. We substitute dry vermouth with dry Spanish sherry (fino or manzanilla) and then toast our own folk heroes, such as José Martí, Simón Bolívar, and Pancho Villa.

3 ounces Scotch whiskey, such as Dewar's
1 ounce dry sherry
Manzanilla olive

Pour the Scotch and sherry into a rocks glass filled with ice. Garnish with the olive.

PEANUT SAUCES ARE POPULAR IN MANY PARTS OF LATIN AMERICA, but especially in Ecuador, where I first tasted this one, served with with fried potato cakes. In neighboring Peru, both chicken and rabbit are prepared in a creamy peanut sauce. In fact, the peanut is believed to have originated in Peru, where it formed part of ancient Inca cuisine.

The peanuts should be ground in a food processor. The dip may be made a day ahead. It can accompany most raw vegetables, such as peppers and radishes. For our party, we served it with a plateful of baby carrots and celery sticks. It was the ideal balance to fried arepas and creamy chocolate flan.

This recipe will make about 2 cups.

GARDEN VEGETABLES WITH CHUNKY PEANUT DIP

One 16-ounce bag baby carrots
1 pound celery, stalks cut into 2-inch sticks

DIP

3 tablespoons vegetable oil
1 medium Spanish onion, finely chopped
1 jalapeño pepper or other hot pepper (such as mirasol), seeded and finely chopped
2 garlic cloves, minced
4 ripe plum tomatoes, peeled, seeded, and chopped
1 cup (about 3 ounces) finely ground, salted cocktail peanuts
2 teaspoons sugar
1 teaspoon salt
Freshly ground black pepper to taste

Heat the oil in a cast-iron or other heavy skillet. When hot, sauté the onion and pepper over medium heat until just softened, about 2 minutes. Add the garlic, tomatoes, ground peanuts, and sugar, and cook over low heat for about 10 minutes. Season with salt and pepper to taste.

ISABEL AND HER HUSBAND COOKED UP this empanada recipe after returning from a trip to Buenos Aires. She is known to bring these to housewarming parties. These bite-sized empanadas, made with frozen puff pastry, are easy to prepare. Eat them warm or at room temperature. They may be made up to two days ahead, refrigerated, and warmed in a 300°F oven before serving.

This makes 36 bite-sized empanadas.

6 garlic cloves, minced
⅓ cup fresh, finely chopped cilantro
½ Spanish onion, finely chopped
Juice of 1 lime
Juice of 1 lemon
1 tablespoon cumin powder
1 teaspoon cracked red pepper
1 teaspoon salt
One 14-ounce can crushed tomatoes
Few drops of hot pepper sauce (optional)
1 tablespoon olive oil
1 pound fresh turkey
1 tablespoon salt
1 tablespoon sugar
Two 17.3-ounce packages frozen
    puff pastry sheets, thawed
36 small Spanish manzanilla olives stuffed
    with pimientos
1 large egg

isabel's
flaky
turkey
empanadas

In a bowl, combine the first ten ingredients to make a tomato salsa. Set aside.

Heat the olive oil in a skillet over medium-high heat. Cook the turkey until it lightly browns, about 5 minutes. Lower the heat and add the salsa and the salt. Simmer on low-medium for 10 to 15 minutes, allowing some of the liquid to reduce. Remove from the heat and stir in the sugar.

Preheat the oven to 400°F.

On a floured surface, lay out one pastry sheet at a time. Using a pastry cutter or blunt knife, cut pastry sheets into 3 × 3-inch squares. Spoon 1 tablespoon of the turkey filling in the center of one square and top with an olive. Fold it into a triangle, pressing the edges together with fork tines. Repeat with the remaining pastry squares.

Arrange all the triangles on an ungreased cookie sheet.

Make an egg wash by beating the egg in a small bowl with 1 tablespoon water. Brush the tops of the empanadas with the egg wash and then bake them until the tops are golden, about 15 minutes.

WHEN I WAS IN HIGH SCHOOL, my friend Mariella Avenarius's mother always had a bowl of shrimp ceviche in her refrigerator. In Ecuador, they say it cures you of the *chuchaquis,* the "mean reds," a.k.a. a hangover.

While we can't vouch for that, we can tell you that this refreshing dish is always a party favorite. The shrimp needs to marinate and chill for two hours. To save time, make this ceviche a day ahead. In Ecuador, it's traditionally served with popcorn on the side—perfect for an Oscar party.

This recipe will serve 8.

1½ pounds large shrimp (26 to 30 shrimp)
Salt
2 large garlic cloves, peeled
2 bay leaves

MARINADE

1 bunch scallions (about 6), white parts only, chopped
1 red onion, chopped
1½ cups chopped tomatoes, canned or fresh, peeled
¾ cup freshly squeezed lime juice (about 3 limes)
1 cup freshly squeezed orange juice
⅛ to ¼ teaspoon cayenne to taste
Salt and freshly ground black pepper to taste
2 to 2½ tablespoons chopped, fresh cilantro

Popcorn, natural, microwave, or stovetop (optional)

ECUADORIAN
SHRIMP ceviche

Peel and devein the shrimp. In a small pot, boil enough water to cover the shrimp. When the water is boiling, add a small palmful of salt, and then the shrimp, garlic, and bay leaves. When the shrimp turn pink, in about a minute, remove them and drain, reserving ½ cup of the shrimp stock to use in the marinade.

In a large bowl, combine the shrimp stock and all the marinade ingredients, except for the cilantro. Toss in the shrimp, add salt and pepper to taste, and refrigerate, covered, for at least 2 hours.

When ready to serve, sprinkle the fresh cilantro over the ceviche. If desired, make popcorn to serve on the side.

SAFFRON-
POTATO bisque

THIS SOUP WAS ADAPTED FROM a recipe by Karen Snyder-Kadish, one of my cooking instructors in New York City. The first day of her class, I made this silky soup and have included it in my party repertoire ever since.

Saffron is the stigma of the crocus flower and must be picked by hand. Though an expensive spice, a little goes a long way. In fact, this soup requires less than a tablespoon. While traditionally associated with Spanish cuisine, saffron is used in many countries. It gives dishes a distinctive flavor and color. There is no need to buy the most expensive threads for this soup, but do not use powdered saffron, which is usually cut with other spices, like turmeric, and loses its flavor quickly.

For this soup, use starchy potatoes, like russets, or all-purpose ones, like Yukon golds.

This will serve 8 or fill 16 cordial glasses.

2 medium potatoes, diced (about 2 cups)
4 large garlic cloves, peeled and mashed with
    a knife or mallet
Large pinch of saffron threads
1½ teaspoons salt
1⅔ cups milk
⅔ cup heavy cream

In a heavy saucepan combine the potatoes, garlic, saffron, and 2 cups of water. Bring to a boil, add the salt, and simmer partially covered over low-medium heat until the potatoes are tender, about 20 minutes. Remove from the heat, add ⅔ cup of the milk, and blend using a hand-held immersion blender or a food processor. When smooth, mix in the remaining milk and cream with a wooden spoon. Serve warm or chilled.

WHEN I WAS IN THE SECOND GRADE, my mother was completing her medical residency in Miami. Since she was seeing patients late into the evening, I was sent to live with my maternal grandparents in Venezuela.

There I spent many afternoons in my abuela Enriqueta's kitchen, shaping and frying these palm-sized corn cakes. Somehow, I could never—and still can't—shape a smooth arepa. But I've decided that it doesn't matter; the cracks give it a rustic look that I'm rather fond of.

In Venezuela, arepas are eaten at least once a week. They can be stuffed with anything, including black beans, chicken and avocado, *carne mechada* (page 14), or ham and cheese. They are also popular in neighboring Colombia, which has a longstanding rivalry with Venezuela over who makes the best arepas. In El Salvador, they make pupusas, which look like oversized arepas.

Masa harina (precooked white cornmeal) is used to make the arepa dough. The most common Venezuelan brand is called PAN, and the most common Colombian brand is called Masarepa; both are sold in Latin food stores or online.

AREPAS WITH WHITE cheddar cheese

Arepas are traditionally seared in a lightly greased griddle until a crust forms, and then baked in a 350°F oven for 20 minutes. But the way my grandmother and I made them was pan-fried to golden perfection as described below.

Once fried, cut the arepa crosswise, smear on a little butter, and add your favorite filling. For this party, we used white, sharp cheddar cheese. They were unbelievable!

To save time, form the arepa early in the day and leave them out at room temperature, covered in plastic wrap. Fry them when you're ready to eat, as they should be enjoyed warm.

This recipe will make 8 to 10 arepas.

2 tablespoons salt
Pinch of sugar
4 cups masa harina, or any finely ground
    white cornmeal
Vegetable oil for frying
Butter (optional)
8 ounces white cheddar, sliced or shredded

In a large bowl, combine 5 cups lukewarm water, salt, and sugar. Add the masa harina, mixing well with your hands until the dough comes together. If the dough is too dry and does not hold together, add a little more water.

Using the palms of your hands, form small balls of dough, about 2 inches in diameter. Flatten them into 3½-inch disks, about ½ inch wide.

Fill a skillet with a half inch of oil and heat. When the oil is sizzling hot, begin frying the arepas in batches over medium heat, making sure not to crowd the pan, and flipping them over so that both sides turn golden. Lay the fried arepas on a plate lined with paper towels. When cool enough to handle, slice an arepa as you would a bagel, smear on a little butter, if desired, and stuff with cheese. Repeat with each arepa.

FOR THIS OSCAR-WORTHY DESSERT, I've taken the traditional flan, a vanilla-flavored custard enjoyed throughout Latin America, and imbued it with bittersweet chocolate and a hint of orange liqueur.

You will need eight 1-cup, ovenproof ramekins to make this dish as individual servings. The flans may be prepared a day in advance, refrigerated in the ramekins, and covered with foil. Alternatively, the flan may be baked in a 9-inch-round cake pan in a water bath, but you will need to add an extra 20 minutes to the baking time.

2 cups sugar
4 cups whole milk
¼ teaspoon vanilla extract
1 cinnamon stick
1 long orange peel
6 ounces bittersweet chocolate,
    roughly chopped
5 large eggs
2 egg yolks
3 tablespoons orange liqueur,
    such as Cointreau or Grand Marnier

individual chocolate flans

SERVES 8

Preheat the oven to 325°F.

Pour 1 cup of the sugar into the center of a deep saucepan and add ½ cup of water. Stirring occasionally, dissolve the sugar over low heat. Once the sugar dissolves, raise the temperature and bring to a boil, and then simmer, without stirring, for 15 to 20 minutes, or until the caramel syrup turns a light amber color. Remove from the heat and quickly divide the caramel into eight 1-cup ramekins, swirling it around to evenly coat the sides and bottom. Set aside.

In a large saucepan, bring the milk, vanilla, cinnamon stick, and orange peel to a rolling boil. Turn the heat off and stir in the chocolate with a spatula or wooden spoon until it has melted.

In a bowl, whisk together the eggs, yolks, orange liqueur, and the remaining cup of sugar. Slowly pour the chocolate mixture into the bowl in a steady stream while whisking constantly. Strain the flan mixture through a sieve into a pitcher, discarding the cinnamon stick and orange peel.

Fill the caramel-coated ramekins with the chocolate flan mixture and place inside a roasting pan filled with a couple of inches of water. Lay a piece of aluminum foil over the top and bake for about an hour. The flan is ready when it is no longer wobbly, or when a toothpick inserted in the center comes out clean.

Carefully remove the roasting pan from the oven, uncover the flans, and cool to room temperature. Chill in the ramekins before serving.

When ready to serve the flans, place individual ramekins in a bowl of hot water for a few seconds to loosen up the flans, then invert each one onto a dessert plate.

clam up

We picked up a few large shells from the local craft store, washed them, spooned in small portions of our ceviche and arranged them on a tray. Polished medium to large scallop, clam, and abalone shells make ideal mini-plates.

cup of soup

Serve appetizer amounts of soups in cordial or port glasses. At Sami's, clear and curvy port glasses from Williams-Sonoma added flair to the presentation of the Saffron-Potato Bisque. They turned out to be the perfect serving size, too—about a half cup. And you won't need spoons.

religious candles

Huge murals of La Virgen de Guadalupe, Mexico's patron saint, are a common sight in Los Angeles. One we spotted by the Olvera marketplace was illuminated by hundreds of religious candles. These votives often portray a religious figure on the front and a prayer on the back, and are lit to honor Jesus or a disciple, a saint, or a loved one. Some are lit to help fulfill a prayer. We also like to display them at parties, either grouped together as a centerpiece on a table or scattered around a room. You can find religious votives online or at Mexican herb stores called *yerberías,* or Caribbean apothecaries, *botánicas.*

tequila tips

There are no worms in tequila. Worms can be found in tequila's cousin, mezcal. Though there are four types of tequila, not all are meant to be drunk as shots or mixed in cocktails. Añejo tequila, for example, is aged in oak barrels for at least a year and is perfect as an after-dinner drink. Reposados, which are aged for at least two months to a year, are also mellow enough for slow sipping. Blanco (or silver) and joven (or gold) tequilas are good for mixing because they are not aged. Blanco is clear and fresh, while joven is mixed, usually with colorings or flavors. Make sure your tequila is made from 100 percent blue agave. Tequilas that have less might be suitable for cocktails, but because of added coloring and flavors, they are not good for drinking straight.

you're invited

Postcards, especially kitschy ones, make for entertaining and inexpensive party invites. For Sami's shindig, we used glamorous movie postcards from the golden age of Mexican cinema. During the 1940s, Mexico City produced remarkable and important films, and two of my favorite actresses became worldwide phenoms during that era: Dolores del Río, who shined as saintly María Candelaria, and María Félix, who epitomized pure evil as the nasty yet gorgeous landowner Doña Bárbara.

BEATS

With the Mexican rock scene finally going from bit player to star billing, we tapped into some of our favorite funk, alterna-rock bands, like Kinky and Molotov. Then it was onto the rock, hip-hop, cumbia-induced sounds of L.A.-based Ozomatli and the guitar tunes of Texan breathren Henry, JoJo, and Ringo of Los Lonely Boys. At the end of the night it was time to pay homage to the master Mexican guitarist, Carlos Santana.

Atlas   Kinky
Ozomatli
Dance and Dense Denso   Molotov
Los Lonely Boys
The Best of Santana

carnival:

our ode to brazil

DINNER AND DANCING FOR 4 OR MORE

BRAZIL IS THE HOME OF CARNIVAL AND CAIPIRINHAS, SAMBA AND SOME OF THE SEXIEST PEOPLE IN THE WORLD,

including two of our friends, Jayma Cordosa and Catia Silva. These two Brazilian beauties, from Curitiba and São Paulo respectively, have been whooping it up and putting together whoop-worthy parties in New York City since 1998, when they met while studying at Fordham University. They started cohosting Brazilian bashes at some of the hottest clubs in New York, supplying samba soundtracks, live drummers, and feather-costumed dancers. Their boisterous evenings became so popular that soon they were hosting events in the Hamptons, Miami, Las Vegas, and Los Angeles. We met the duo at one of their New York parties. The timing could not have been better, as Carolina and I had been eager to throw a Carnival celebration for a few years, but since neither of us has ever been to Carnival, we didn't know where to begin. Now we had Jayma and Catia to be our cohosts and Carnival experts.

As our guest list grew we needed to find a space that was big enough. The four of us settled on the tropical LQ (Latin Quarter) club in midtown Manhattan. It has great Latin details such as big palm trees and also a small stage and a sunken dance floor for optimum viewing of the samba dancers. The guest list included Brazilian expats, as well as friends from the Dominican Republic, Panama, Chile, Honduras, and Puerto Rico. The only requirement? That everyone come ready to eat bold Brazilian-inspired food and then dance the night away. Jayma and Catia hired professional Carnival dancers, played Brazilian beats, and served their country's national cocktail, the caipirinha, and *Capeta Batida,* a powerful guaraná brew that in Portuguese means the "Devil's Shake."

The dancers shimmied in their sequined bikinis and plumaged headdresses, teaching us all how to samba. We tried our best to keep up while wearing gorgeous candy-colored gowns by Brazilian designer Carlos Miele, a good friend of Jayma's, and even a few of her own designs— slinky, cut-down-to-there, slit-up-to-here black dresses.

To complete the Carnival motif, we wore multicolored Mardi Gras baubles from Cartier, a generous loan from a friend who works there. The jewels, like the dancers, were a huge success. After our traditional dinner, the dancers, drummers, and drinks had us doing the devil's shake all night long.

CAIPIRINHA

SERVES I

LIMES MAKE THIS DRINK SLIGHTLY SOUR RATHER THAN SWEET. If you don't have cachaça, substitute vodka *(caipriroska)* or light rum *(caipirissima)*. Jayma's and Catia's favorite brands of cachaça are Pitú, Beleza Pura, and Velho Barrero. Since cachaça is made from sugarcane, use cut raw sugarcane as stirrers. Look for sugarcane at gourmet grocery stores, farmer's markets, and online.

1 lime, quartered
1 tablespoon sugar
2 ounces cachaça
4 large ice cubes

Place the lime quarters in an old-fashioned glass. Add in the sugar and mash. Pour in the cachaça and add the ice cubes. Give it a stir and enjoy!

Devil's Shake

CAPETA batida

SERVES 2

TALK ABOUT AN ADULT SPIN ON A CHILDREN'S CLASSIC. This drink tastes like lightly spiked chocolate milk. In addition to instant chocolate-milk mix, it calls for guaraná powder, which comes from a berry grown in Brazil and Venezuela and is sold in health food stores as an energy supplement. In Brazil, a popular soft drink is made from guaraná. The *Capeta Batida* tastes great with or without it, so no worries if you can't find it. Watch out with this one—after the sugar, chocolate, caffeine, and alcohol buzz wears off, you might be ready for the devil to claim your soul.

1 teaspoon guaraná powder
1 teaspoon instant chocolate-milk mix,
    such as Nestlé or Quik
1 teaspoon ground cinnamon
1 ounce milk
½ cup sweetened condensed milk
2 ounces cachaça

Combine all the ingredients in a shaker filled with ice. Shake vigorously and strain into chilled martini glasses.

LQ blast

SERVES 2

SOME OF THE BEST LATIN DRINKS, music, and dancing in New York City can be found in this subterranean lounge, LQ (Latin Quarter). This is the club's signature drink.

4 ounces pineapple juice
3 ounces dark rum
1 ounce light rum
1 ounce Blue Curaçao
2 pineapple wedges
2 mango wedges

Combine all the ingredients, except the pineapple and mango, in a shaker filled with ice. Shake and strain into martini glasses and garnish each with a pineapple and mango wedge.

PISCO sour

SERVES 2

THIS CLASSIC COCKTAIL FROM PERU AND CHILE is made with pisco, a potent, clear Peruvian grape brandy. Capel Alto de Carmen and Don César are brands to look for. Traditionally, this drink is made with Chilean or Brazilian lemons, which are quite sour and hard to find in the States, so we substitute regular lemons. For a festive presentation, rim the glasses with sugar before serving. Skip the sugar altogether if you prefer a more sour (and margarita-like) drink. You can also skip the egg, which is mainly there to create a pretty froth.

4 ounces fresh lemon juice (4 to 6 lemons)
2 tablespoons superfine sugar
1 egg white
⅔ cup pisco

Combine all the ingredients in a shaker filled with ice. Shake vigorously and strain into sugar-rimmed sherry glasses.

PISCO sweet

SERVES 6

FOR THOSE WHO DON'T LIKE SOUR DRINKS, here's a sweet pisco alternative that a Peruvian family friend makes by the pitcher for her get-togethers.

6 tablespoons superfine sugar
4 cups fresh strawberries, hulled and quartered
1 cup evaporated milk
2 cups pisco
4 cups ice
6 strawberries, for garnish

Combine the sugar, strawberries, milk, and pisco in a blender and pulse until smooth. Add the ice and blend until liquefied. Serve in tall glasses and garnish each one with a strawberry.

FRIED
GREEN
TOMATOES
WITH spicy aïoli

THE FIRST TIME I MET my husband's family in North Carolina, his mother prepared a plate of fried green tomatoes. Years later, at a party in Miami, my Cuban friend Mario Garcia served a plate of these with Spanish aïoli. Taking a cue from him, Isabel and I have since been serving these Southern fritters with a Latin twist.

Look for green tomatoes that are bright and firm, with no obvious bruising. Once fried, serve immediately.

This recipe makes about 22 fried tomato slices.

4 large green tomatoes, cut into ½-inch slices
1¼ cups buttermilk
1 cup stone-ground cornmeal
1 cup all-purpose flour
1 teaspoon salt
1 teaspoon sugar
About ½ cup vegetable or canola oil
Kosher salt (optional)
¼ teaspoon cayenne powder
Aïoli (page 80)

In a bowl, soak the tomato slices in the buttermilk for 10 to 15 minutes. You may need to weigh them down with a small plate.

In a shallow bowl, whisk together the cornmeal, flour, salt, and sugar.

Heat the oil in a large cast-iron skillet or heavy sauté pan over medium-high heat. When the oil is hot, dredge both sides of a tomato slice in the cornmeal mixture and fry each side over medium-high heat. (To test that the oil is hot enough, lightly touch the oil with the edge of a cornmeal-coated tomato slice; if it sizzles, the oil is ready.)

Fry the tomatoes in batches, filling up the skillet, but be careful to leave about a half inch between the tomato slices.

Once the tomatoes are fried to a golden color, 2 to 3 minutes per side, carefully lay them on top of a plate lined with paper towels. Sprinkle with kosher salt, if desired.

Before serving, fold ¼ teaspoon of cayenne into the aïoli.

Serve the tomatoes warm, alongside the spicy aïoli.

MOQUECA

BRAZIL IS A COUNTRY WITH MANY REGIONAL CUISINES. For our entrée, Isabel and I decided on this hearty seafood stew from the Bahia region of Brazil, north of Rio de Janeiro. Served with a side of rice, it is reminiscent of Spanish paella but with African and Portuguese influences.

A classic moqueca calls for dende oil, a reddish oil extracted from the African palm, and fiery malagueta peppers. Since these are difficult to find, we substitute olive oil mixed with a pinch of paprika and jalapeños. The success of this fish stew depends on buying the freshest seafood available. Cooking time is swift; once ready, the moqueca should be served *depressa,* which means "quickly" in Portuguese.

This will serve 4.

1 pound large shrimp (18 to 20), peeled and
     deveined, shells reserved
Juice of 2 limes
1½ pounds orange roughy, cod, or other
     whitefish, cut into 2- to 4-inch cubes
4 tablespoons olive oil
1 large red onion, minced
3 large garlic cloves, minced
2 jalapeño or other hot peppers, cored,
     seeded, and minced
3 medium ripe tomatoes, chopped;
     or 1½ cups chopped, drained canned
     tomatoes, about one 14-ounce can
1⅓ cups coconut milk
2 teaspoons cumin
Salt and freshly ground black pepper to taste
16 to 20 mussels, scrubbed and debearded
4 tablespoons olive oil, stained with a pinch
     of paprika
4 tablespoons roughly chopped cilantro,
     leaves and stems

Place the shrimp in a bowl with half the lime juice. Fill a small saucepan with the reserved shrimp shells and enough water to cover them. Bring to a boil, reduce the heat, and simmer until the water reduces to about a cup, about 20 minutes.

Place the fish in another bowl with the remaining lime juice.

Heat the olive oil in a Dutch oven or other large, sturdy pot over medium heat. Add the onion, garlic, and peppers, and sauté until the onion is tender, about 5 minutes. Add the tomatoes, stirring gently for about 5 minutes.

Stir in the coconut milk, the reserved shrimp broth, and cumin. Lower the heat, cover, and simmer for 10 minutes. Season with salt and pepper to taste.

Add the mussels and simmer for 3 minutes, covered. Then add the fish cubes, cover, and simmer another 5 minutes. Finally, add the shrimp and cook covered another 3 minutes, or until the shrimp and fish are done, making sure not to overcook either. Stir in the spiced oil, cilantro, and salt and pepper to taste. Remove from the heat. Discard any mussels that have not opened. Serve with rice on the side.

RICE WITH
PECANS AND cherries

THIS VIVACIOUS VARIATION ON THE standard Brazilian side of white rice pairs well with the moqueca. Use a starchier, medium-grain rice, such as the type used in Spanish paellas. Since cooking times and the amount of liquid needed for each brand of rice varies, make sure to read the package directions. When serving, spoon some of the moqueca's coconut sauce over the rice, if desired.

This will serve 4.

Extra virgin olive oil
1 garlic clove, minced
Salt to taste
1 cup medium-grain rice
½ cup dried cherries
½ cup coarsely chopped pecans
Handful of chopped parsley

Heat the oil in a small saucepan over medium heat. Sauté the garlic until it starts to turn golden. Add 1½ cups water and bring to a boil. When the water boils, add a small palmful of salt and the rice. Reduce the heat to low, cover, and simmer for 16 to 18 minutes, or until the water is absorbed and the rice is tender. Remove from the heat, add the dried cherries, pecans, and parsley directly into the saucepan, over the rice. Cover to trap the steam. After 3 minutes, stir the rice, fluff with a fork, and serve.

WHILE IN PARTS OF THE South collards are cooked long and slow, in Brazil they are sautéed fast and furious, resulting in a crisp texture and a hearty flavor. This recipe is a classic side dish from the Brazilian state of Minas Gerais, which is famous for its Afro-Latin cooking. Collards pair wonderfully with the moqueca.

This will serve 4.

1½ pounds fresh collard greens,
    halved lengthwise, stems and center ribs
    discarded
4 bacon strips
2 garlic cloves, mashed
Salt

collard greens, minas gerais style

Stack the greens and cut crosswise into 1½-inch strips.

Heat a cast-iron or other heavy skillet and cook the bacon strips until crisp, about 5 minutes. Transfer the bacon strips to a paper towel–lined plate.

Remove all but approximately 1 tablespoon of the bacon fat from the skillet.

Over medium heat, sauté the garlic. The second it starts to turn golden, add the greens. Sauté the greens using tongs to occasionally turn them over for even cooking. After a couple of minutes they will be a bright green color. Remove them from the heat, place in a serving bowl, season with salt, and crumble the bacon slices over the top.

Toss gently and serve warm.

PRETTY PASSION fruit mousse

PASSION FRUIT HAS AN UNMISTAKABLE flowery aroma and a tart flavor often tempered with sugar. It reminds me of summer vacations in Venezuela. My grandmother would serve halved passion fruits for breakfast, sprinkled with raw sugar. With little coffee spoons we drank down the yellow gelatinous pulp with its edible black seeds.

The passion fruit is native to southern Brazil, Paraguay, and northern Argentina, though other varieties come from Australia and Polynesia. The name is a reference to the fruit tree's beautiful white and purple flowers, which Portuguese missionaries in Brazil believed symbolized the Passion of the Christ. In other parts of Latin America, it is called *parchita* and *maracuyá*.

In this simple dessert, passion fruit pulp is whipped into a creamy mousse and drizzled with a honeylike glaze, a concoction created by Peruvian caterer Mariella Hurtado, who started her baking career at the Lawn Tennis Country Club in Lima, Peru.

Goya and other brands sell frozen (unsweetened) passion fruit pulp in 14-ounce packages. You will need a little more than a package for this recipe. Leftover pulp may be turned into juice by adding water and sugar. If you can't find passion fruit pulp, then sweetened passion fruit juice is a fine substitute. Make sure the juice is sweetened with sugar or corn syrup and not with other juices like apple. As a substitute, boil 2¼ cups of the sweetened passion fruit juice until is reduced to 1¼ cups, and omit the sugar. If using juice for the glaze, use the same quantity of juice and sugar as the recipe calls for.

This mousse may be made up to one day in advance and set in a large serving bowl or in individual bowls. The glaze may also be made ahead and spooned decoratively over the mousse before serving.

This dessert serves 8 to 10.

PASSION FRUIT MOUSSE

1¼ cups frozen passion fruit pulp, thawed
1 cup sugar
2 packages gelatin powder
1 pint heavy cream, chilled

GLAZE

2 tablespoons cornstarch or arrowroot
1 cup passion fruit pulp
⅓ cup sugar

In a small saucepan, stir the 1¼ cups of thawed passion fruit pulp and sugar together over low heat, until the sugar dissolves. In a ¼ cup of cold water, dissolve the gelatine and add to the saucepan, stirring until combined. Do not bring to a boil. Remove from the heat and let cool.

In a mixing bowl, whip the heavy cream until stiff peaks form. In a steady stream, add the passion fruit mixture to the heavy cream and mix on low speed for a few seconds until it is all incorporated and the mousse turns a light yellow-orange color.

Pour the mousse into a serving bowl to set. Chill for at least 4 hours or overnight.

To make the glaze, dissolve the cornstarch in 4 tablespoons cold water. In a saucepan, heat 1 cup of the passion fruit pulp and sugar, stirring until the sugar dissolves. Add the dissolved cornstarch and simmer, stirring constantly. Once the glaze is thick enough to coat a wooden spoon, 2 to 3 minutes, remove from the heat. Let cool and refrigerate.

To decorate your guests' dessert plates, consider filling a plastic squeeze bottle with the glaze. These are sold in kitchen supply, beauty, or craft stores.

leaf it to me

Not everything has to come up roses. For this party, we decided to forgo flower decor for vibrant green leaf arrangements. More than dainty flowers, leaves are unexpected and add an element of drama. Buy them at florists and nurseries. For strong visual statements, the bigger the leaf, the better. Feel free to mix and match different varieties.

pining away

Ever wonder why so many home accents have pineapple detailing? In addition to being a good-looking fruit, the prickly treat symbolizes hospitality. Since the fruit is native to parts of Brazil, we included a bunch on the tables at our party. They also make great candleholders when you cut them in half, core them, and place a votive candle inside. Keep the fruit from turning dull yellow or brown by rubbing half a lemon on the exposed flesh.

dancers and dressing

To hire professional dancers for your next party, call the local ballroom dance studio for students or teachers who perform at events. Post a request for Latin dancers in local Latin community-service organizations. Call a costume rental store to find a collection of Carnival outfits for guys and girls.

aguardiente

Aguardiente, which means "burning water" or "fire water," refers to a nearly pure-alcohol spirit made from sugarcane and includes cachaça from Brazil and grape brandy piscos from Peru, Chile, and Bolivia. Popular mixed drinks in these countries often call for cachaça or pisco, but in Ecuador and Colombia they drink aguardiente straight. In Colombia, the alcohol is a national symbol, with poems and songs honoring it. As the name suggests, it's very potent, and when Colombia was under Spanish rule, the king once tried, unsuccessfully, to outlaw it.

BEATS

Jayma and Catia put together our soundtrack. They looked to Bebel, João Gilberto's progeny, for smooth bossa beats to start the evening. Then they pulled out some famous Brazilian DJ compilations for the dancing. Jayma also introduced us to sexy Ivete Sangalo and her Brazilian Axé sound, an addictive musical mixture of samba, rock, African drumming, and reggae. As night folded into early morning, we played the sultry sounds of Brazilian legend Caetano Veloso and the spirited songs of Capo Verde's Cesaria Evora.

Tanto Tempo   Bebel Gilberto
Volumes 2 and *3-Mix Show*   Felipe Venancio
Beat Beleza   Ivete Sangalo
Miss Perfumado   Cesaria Evora
The Best of Caetano Veloso

La Dulce Vida at Vizcaya

Vizcaya Museum and Gardens: www.vizcayamuseum.org
Narciso Rodriguez: www.narcisorodriguez.com
Fans: www.boutique-flamenco.com; www.crazyforspain.com
Cigars: www.cigar.com

Guayaberas:
La Casa de las Guayaberas
5840 SW 8th St.
West Miami, FL 33144-5051
305-266-9683

Kumquats: www.kumquatgrowers.com
Sugarcane: www.cubanfoodmarket.com
Spanish sherry: www.tienda.com

Victor's Café
236 West 52nd St.
New York, NY 10019
212-586-7714
www.victorscafe.com

Latina Ladies Who Lunch

Spanish playing cards: www.newtonsnovelties.com
Juices: www.cubanfoodmarket.com
Malta: www.mexgrocer.com
Cuban crackers: www.cubanfoodmarket.com

Paladar
161 Ludlow St.
New York, NY 10002
212-473-3535

Horsing Around La Pampa

Estancia el Rocío: www.estanciaelrocio.com
Latin wine: www.vinoconvida.com; www.dolium.com; www.cousinomacul.com;
        www.santo-tomas.com; www.chateau-camou.com.mx; www.robledofamilywinery.com
Stamps: www.rubberstampchamp.com
Pablo Ramirez: www.pabloramirez.com.ar

A Pool Party in Puerto Rico

Edmundo Castillo: www.edmundocastillo.com
Sushi plates: www.pearlriver.com
Water Club: www.waterclubsanjuan.com
Coconut water: www.vitacoco.com

Celebrating Mexico: Art, Food, and Culture

Sully Bonnelly: www.sullybonnelly.com
Muros Museum: www.muros.org.mx
Corn husks: www.mexgrocer.com
Mexican paper flowers: www.latinworks.com
Lotería cards: www.latinworks.com
Hosteria and Spa Las Quintas: www.hlasquintas.com
Salts: www.salttraders.com
Hibiscus tea: www.theteastore.com

Turning Up the Heat in the Hamptons

Carmen Marc Valvo: www.carmenmarcvalvo.com
Seashells: www.seashellworld.com
Carmen wine: www.carmen.com
Personalized wine labels: www.winegiftclub.com

Alta Cocina

¡Hola! magazine: www.hola.com
Turrón: www.tienda.com
Agustín Reyes: www.agustinreyes.com
Nenuco: www.tienda.com
Maracas: www.musichouseshop.com

Romance in La Romana: *Un Paso Doble*

Casa de Campo: www.hotelcasadecampo.com
Oscar de la Renta: www.oscardelarenta.com
American Ballet Theatre: www.abt.org
Cava: www.winesfromspain.com

Los Angeles: An Oscar Party in the Hollywood Hills

Carolina Herrera: www.carolinaherrera.com
Port glasses: www.williams-sonoma.com
Olvera Street: www.olvera-street.com
Religious candles: www.churchcandlesonline.com

Carnival: Our Ode to Brazil

Carlos Miele: www.carlosmiele.com.br

LQ (Latin Quarter)
511 Lexington Ave.
New York, NY 10017
212-593-7575

Cartier (Delice de Goa line): www.cartier.com
Carnival costumes: www.arara.biz

The Pantry

Here are a few of our favorite on- and off-line places for finding and ordering Latin ingredients and other necessities.

Kitchen Market
218 Eighth Ave.
New York, NY 10011
888-HOT-4433
www.kitchenmarket.com
Peruvian mirasol peppers, chiles, huitlacoche, precooked white cornmeal for arepas, dulce de leche, cajeta

MexGrocer
7445 Girard Ave.
Suite 6
La Jolla, CA 92037
858-459-0577
www.mexgrocer.com
Huitlacoche, achiote paste, chiles

La Tienda
www.tienda.com
Chorizos, Spanish smoked paprika, boquerones, wide variety of Spanish olives

Kalustyan's
123 Lexington Ave.
New York, NY 10016
800-352-3451
www.kalustyans.com
Canned and dried chiles, guava paste, guava, guanabana (soursop), pomegranate molasses

Penzeys Spices
P.O. Box 924
Brookfield, WI 53008
800-741-7787
www.penzeys.com
Large selection of spices from around the world

Latino Deli
253 West 28th St. #4
New York, NY 10001
212-629-7433
www.latinodeli.com
Variety of Latin cheeses and ingredients

Cuban Food Market
877-999-9945
www.cubanfoodmarket.com
Guava paste, guava shells

Conchita
www.conchita-foods.com
Guava paste, guava shells

Dean and Deluca
560 Broadway
New York, NY 10012
800-221-7714
www.deandeluca.com
Chiles, spices, cheeses, specialty oils

I Gourmet
877-IGOURMET
www.igourmet.com
Cheeses from Spain, South America, and Central America

Marky's Caviar
687 NE 79th St.
Miami, FL 33183
800-722-8427
www.markys.com

El Rey Chocolates
www.chocolates-elrey.com
Fine Venezuelan chocolate

index

(Page numbers in *italic* refer to illustrations.)